DEVOTIONALS *for* Mommy & Me

SECRETS SAVORED

Secrets Savored Inc.

Mommy & Me

....

Requests for information should be addressed to:
Secrets Savored Inc.
P.O. Box 2257
Cordova, Tennessee 38088

....

To Order the Mommy & Me devotional book: Access Secrets Savored web-site at secretssavored.org.

Dedication

She had very little as a young wife and mother of 12 children. The little white framed house was barren compared to homes these days. A sofa, side chair, and two end tables were in the living room, and a bed and dresser in each bedroom. There were no accessories to speak of and just a small table in the kitchen.

Grandma Cleckner was a beautiful woman with long white hair that was French braided down her back. She was bedridden due to a stroke; her children cared for her. As a child, I would stand at a distance watching my aunts and uncles carry her to the bathroom to care for her personal needs. She was always joyful in spite of her circumstances.

Grandma Cleckner realized her great need for a Savior and taught her twelve children the ways of God and the truths of His Word. I was never allowed to speak with her. I wish I had been able to sit and talk with her. I am quite certain that God would have been at the center of our conversations. She had very little but somehow I think it was okay because she had what mattered most. She had Christ and He was enough! This book is dedicated to Grandma Cleckner—mommy of 12!

Contents

These commandments I give you today are to be on your hearts...

Talk about them when you sit at home and when you walk along the road, when you lie down and when you get up...

Write them on the doorframes of your houses and on your gates.

DEUTERONOMY 6:5-9

Acknowledgements

I want to thank the eleven creative and gifted young moms who worked tirelessly writing these truths from God's Word. They were written from hearts that desire to help other young mommies fulfill the mandate given to all parents in Deuteronomy 6. This *Mommy and Me* devotional book has been a collective effort and I want to thank Emily Black, Laura Dawkins, Rachel Mason, Kathryn Mayo, Jennie McKay, Erin Mullen, Libby Phillips, Christy Pritchard, Dorie Pyron, Amy Rogers and Jenny Triplett for believing in this project and in a God who blesses obedience.

To our daughter, Angela Porada, and her dear friends, Jenna Gassid and Amanda Savage: Thank you for writing the Along the Way section of this book. I am blessed and challenged by the way you three mommies live out your faith and teach your children Along the Way. You are admired and appreciated!

To our Secrets Savored Board: I am grateful for your prayers, faithful service, and encouragement. This book is an answer to our prayers. May God use it for His glory and honor!

To Marge Lenow: My dear friend and mentor thank you for tireless hours of editing, and the days and nights spent in my office trying to meet a deadline. As always, you do all things well. I am grateful for you—and indebted to you!

To Amanda Weaver: You have been a blessing from the first day we met to consider graphics for the Secrets curriculum. You are a precious and gifted young woman who has allowed God to use your gifts and abilities. I am thankful for all the hours you have spent creating beautiful works that are a blessing to others. You are special!

To Jenny Triplett: You have been such a wonderful blessing in my life. There cannot be a greater administrative assistant anywhere! Thank you for catching all the balls I was dropping while working on *Mommy and Me*. You are a very efficient young woman and a special gift to me!

To the Bellevue Secrets Leadership: Ladies, you have been such an encouragement to me. Several of you have been with me from the beginning of Secrets Savored, others of you joined as the years progressed. Thank you for praying for and believing in this ministry. I am grateful for your desire to live out Titus 2 by investing your lives in the lives of young women. You bless me!

To Cheri, Ginger, Cathy, Jennie and Susan: You are my special heart friends who have walked this road of suffering with me. Thank you for all the calls, texts, prayers and words of encouragement. You will never know this side of heaven what a blessing you have been to me. I love you!

To our younger daughter, Kelly: You live out the love of Christ every day in the way you love your family and others! What a joy you are!

To my husband, Mark, who spends these days bound to a bed due to Multiple Systems Atrophy: In spite of your illness, you continually exude the love, joy and peace of Christ. You have believed in me and God's calling on my life—never allowing me to quit. Your prayers have sustained me. Thank you for setting such an incredible example of faithfulness and obedience to our Lord. You are a man of prayer, committing to spend these last days of confinement praying tirelessly for family, friends, this ministry and the lost. You are a treasure and I will forever thank God for placing this 15 year old young lady in your sights—and in your heart. I love you with all that I am!

And to my Heavenly Father who has been so very faithful these past few years: He has walked this road of suffering with us and has never failed us! He has met every need and has given peace, joy and even laughter to our home. May You, Lord, be glorified in the pages of this book, and may You change the hearts and lives of mommies and children through the truth of Your Word!

Foreword

My husband, Mark, and I grew up going to church, but we spent the first eleven years of our marriage running from the Lord. We ran after *money*, *possessions* and *position*, which eventually led to an empty life and marriage. But, on April 14, 1984, God miraculously saved my husband and my marriage. In June of that year, because of the light Mark's new found faith was shining upon the darkness in my life, I gave my heart to Christ. Our marriage relationship and our parenting changed dramatically and became Christ-focused and Spirit-led for the first time.

Parenting can be hard and very exhausting. Up until the time Mark was saved, I felt as if I were a single parent. Due to the fact that he was chasing hard after success, he was home very little and was unengaged in raising our girls. It was a lonely time for me. I longed to have a partner to share the joys and frustrations in raising Angela and Kelly. I desired to have a spiritual leader to guide me and the girls.

When Mark was saved, the changes were immediately apparent. When he arrived home the night of April 14th, he was holding a bouquet of flowers. Now, that was something new! The next morning was Sunday and he suggested we go to church and then offered to help get the girls dressed. That was also something new.

After church, he assisted with lunch and suggested that we all go for a walk. Something new again!! Once we arrived home, I took Kelly upstairs for her nap. I could hear music coming from the den downstairs. As I got to the bottom of the staircase, I realized that the song was a Christmas song—in April. The album he was playing was the *only* Christian one we had in our home. Mark was lying on the couch, and as I glanced down, he had tears falling from his cheeks. He asked me to sit down because he had something to tell me. Mark told me that he had given his heart to Christ. Now remember, I was a *church* girl and I thought I was a *good* person. I also thought all our problems were Mark's fault! So, while I welcomed this new man, I in no way felt I was a "sinner in need of a Savior."

The first and most powerful change in Mark was his desire to know God. He discovered that to know Him, he had to be in the Word. So, he went out and purchased a new Bible. Night after night, week after week, he would lie on the couch reading it. He began attending a weekly Bible study. God was changing my husband from the inside out. I loved this new godly man who was leading me and our girls spiritually. Because of the light shining through his new life, I gave my heart to Christ—and when I did everything changed!

The foundation of our home was now secure! Before Christ, we were building on *sand*—the things of the world. But, after being saved, Jesus Christ and His Word became the foundation we desired to build our home upon. For the very first time since saying, "I do" on July 19, 1973, we were of one flesh, heart, mind and spirit. Our parenting changed because God's Word was our main source of wisdom and direction in raising our girls.

As parents, one of our main responsibilities is to teach our children. The Hebrew word for parents is *horim* from a root word meaning *teacher*. We are not to rely on churches or Christian schools to teach our children biblical truths—we are to teach them. God designed it this way. In the book of Deuteronomy, we see God's instructions to parents as to their responsibility in the teaching of His Word.

Mommy and Me was written by moms who understand that in this hectic, calendar–filled life, it is difficult to find the time to impart Biblical truths to your children. In an effort to help you as a mom teach your children and fulfill Deuteronomy 6:4-9, this resource was created.

Before you begin to utilize this material, consider the words of admonishment Moses gave to parents: He encouraged them to "**Love the LORD YOUR GOD WITH ALL YOUR HEART AND WITH ALL YOUR SOUL AND WITH ALL YOUR STRENGTH.**" His commandments are to be "**on your hearts.**" Before Mark and I were saved, we did not know Jesus or His Word. Therefore, we had nothing worthwhile to teach our girls from a biblical perspective. Parents cannot teach what they have not experienced or what they do not know. In order to impart biblical truths and set an example of loving Christ with all your heart, soul and strength, you must come to the place we came to—accepting Christ as your personal Lord and Savior. Do not go any further in this book without making that vital life–changing decision. I am eternally grateful that God changed our home, lives, marriage and parenting through changing our hearts!

In order to help you "**impress them on your children**" and to "**talk about them when you sit at home**," we have provided twelve weekly devotionals on various topics. The topics include: friendship, self-control, contentment, respect, forgiveness and many others.

The daily devotions include **Prep for Mom** and **Script for Mom**. The **Prep for Mom** will enable you to adequately prepare for the topic that day. The **Script for Mom** will give you a clear outline for teaching the lesson.

Much of life is "**when you walk along the road**" and "**when you lie down and when you get up**." In today's terms, we might say "as you drive to and from school" and "as you sit at the ball field." For these biblical teaching ideas, which are entitled *Along the Way*, three moms offer suggestions to impart biblical truths and principles to your children in everyday life.

Mom, if you want your children to follow God, it is vital that you make Him a part of your everyday life. You must help your children see God in all aspects of life.

Moses went on to say, "**tie them as symbols on your hands**" and "**bind them on your foreheads**." God's Word is to be as interwoven into the hearts and minds of your children as if it were tied or bound to them.

He ended these verses with "**write them on the doorframes of your houses and on your gates**." Everyone enters and exits a home through a door. When your children come and go from your home, they should be exposed to God's Word. Place scripture in prominent places so that they will have God's Word ever before them. Hang it on walls, write it on black boards, attach it to the side of your refrigerator and place it on the mirror of their bathroom.

The key to teaching our children to love God was simply stated by Moses in these verses. As moms, we must not relegate our God-given responsibility of teaching our children biblical truths and principles to others. Eternal truths are most effectively learned in a loving environment in a Christ–honoring home.

Blessings as you seek to teach your little ones about the One and Only!

Dianne

PART ONE:

Impress them on Your Children

You are...
Special

In this week's *Mommy and Me*, we will be talking about how SPECIAL we are to God. Using Psalm 139, we will learn that God knows us better than anyone else. He is watching over us and we are in His thoughts continually. He made us who we are—on purpose—and He wants us to tell others about Him.

If we try to evaluate ourselves by the world's standard, we will misunderstand our unique design and significance. Sooner or later we will suppose ourselves less than special, allowing ourselves to be wooed away from the life and love our Creator meant for us to enjoy. In this week's devotionals, we want to give the children a very clear picture of who God says they are and how SPECIAL God has made them to be.

You are precious to God. Do not doubt it. He has made you very special.

We want you mommas to be reminded of this, too! You are precious to God. Do not doubt it. He has made you very SPECIAL. He intends for you to know abundant life and intimate love through a relationship with Him. He intends to use His life and love in you to win the hearts of your children.

Before you begin this week's study, go out and buy two small, identical potted plants with lovely little flowers. If your child has a favorite color, get that one. It will be more personal for him! Keep it simple and go cheap. Something really small is all you need.

Ready! Set! You are SPECIAL!

DAY 1

PREP FOR MOM...

Today, we will take a look at the verses in Psalm 139:1-4, which tell us that God knows us better than anyone else. Familiarize yourself with the following scriptures:

Read through Psalm 139. Keep in mind that David wrote this song as a celebration of the excellence of Creator God in both forming and knowing us intentionally and intimately. Letting the weight of this gift of grace settle into our hearts inspires a response. King David is good company for realizing who God is, accepting how much He loves us, and responding with hearts full of praise and integrity.

ACTIVITY PROPS AND SUPPLIES:

- Two small plants
- A wedding picture of you and your husband (grandparents or close friends)

SCRIPT FOR MOM...

Today we are going to talk about God and how well He knows mommy, daddy, and you because He created each of us.

Tell your children the story of how you and your husband met, dated, and got married. Kids love this! Show them a wedding picture and talk about some of your favorite memories from that day. Note: Every family is unique. So, if you would rather not share your personal story, feel free to adapt by telling someone else's marriage story—maybe a family member's story or that of a close friend.

Talk to your children about how well you know your husband. List some of the things you have learned about him—his favorite color, favorite food, favorite movie, his hobbies, the name of his childhood pet, etc.

Question #1: Ask your children what things they have learned about their dad. For little bitty ones, just keep it simple. For example, talk about their favorite things to do with Daddy?

Explain that family members are SPECIAL to one another. They know each other very well because they love each other and spend lots of time together.

We know our friends and our family pretty well don't we? Can you believe that even as well as daddy and I know each other and you and your friends know each other—God knows even more about all of us?

Question #2: What are some things you know about your friend _____?

Explain to your children that God knows us better than anyone else. He knows us better than I know _____ (daddy or family member), or than you know your friends. God knows us inside and out. He knows all the good and all the bad about us...and He still loves us!

Read Psalm 139:1-4 together: "Lord, you have examined me. You know all about me. You know when I sit down and when I get up. You know my thoughts before I think them. You know where I go and where I lie down. You know well everything I do. Lord, even before I say a word, you already know what I am going to say." ICB

These verses tell us that God knows all about us and that we are SPECIAL to Him. He knows what we are doing. He can read our minds, and He knows what we are going to say before we even say it. God is pretty cool!

Tell your children that when you met their daddy:

- You wanted to spend a lot of time with him and get to know him as well as you could.
- God wants us to spend a lot of time with Him and to get to know Him as well as we can, too.

God loves us and accepts us just as we are. Wow! No matter what we do, God loves us and wants to spend time with us! That means we must all be very, very SPECIAL to God!

ACTIVITY:

- Show your children the two flowering plants you purchased.

- Allow them to touch them and smell them—they may even want to give each plant a name.

- Place both pots outside in a sunny spot.

- Each day following, let your children water one plant, but DO NOT water the other.

- This is the mystery we'll uncover as we go throughout this week!

Prayer: *Dear God, thank you for making me* SPECIAL. *I am grateful that You know me and love me, no matter what I do! Help me to learn about You so I can grow up to be like You. Amen!*

DAY 2

PREP FOR MOM...

Today, we will take a look at Psalm 139:5-10. These verses tell us that God is watching over us because we are His and we are SPECIAL to Him. Familiarize yourself with the following scriptures:

"You are all around me—in front and in back. You have put your hand on me. Your knowledge is amazing to me. It is more than I can understand. Where can I go to get away from your Spirit? Where can I run from you? If I go up to the skies, you are there. If I lie down where the dead are, you are there. If I rise with the sun in the east, and settle in the west beyond the sea, even there you would guide me. With your right hand you would hold me." Psalm 139:5-10 ICB

"For you are a holy people, who belong to the LORD your God. Of all the people on earth, the LORD your God has chosen you to be his own SPECIAL treasure." Deuteronomy 7:6 NLT

ACTIVITY PROPS AND SUPPLIES:

- The two small plants from yesterday
- A small object that is special to your child

SCRIPT FOR MOM...

Today we are going to talk about how God watches over us because we are His and we are SPECIAL to Him.

> **Question #1:** Mommy and daddy watch over you, don't we? What are some ways we watch over you?

Talk to your child about a time when he got lost or when you were lost. (Or someone you know)

Discuss how your child felt being lost, who found him, and how seeing a familiar face after being lost made him feel.

Question #2: Did you run and hug the person tightly who found you?

Question #3: Did you know that even though mommy and daddy did not know where you were, God did? He knew right where you were. You were not alone.

Explain that we have all experienced moments of getting lost. Even grown ups can easily get turned around while driving somewhere new. Using the GPS in your car or on your smart phone, explain to your child how this will easily help point you in the right direction.

Read Psalm 139:5-10 together. "You are all around me—in front and in back. You have put your hand on me. Your knowledge is amazing to me. It is more than I can understand. Where can I go to get away from your Spirit? Where can I run from you? If I go up to the skies, you are there. If I lie down where the dead are, you are there. If I rise with the sun in the east, and settle in the west beyond the sea, even there you would guide me. With your right hand you would hold me." ICB

These verses show us that:

- No matter where we are, GOD IS WATCHING OVER US, even in that moment when we feel lost.
- God is guarding us on all sides.
- God will guide us and hug us tightly to help us know the way! What great news!
- All the time, God is watching over us and keeping us safe.

God surely does love us, doesn't He? We are all very, very SPECIAL to God! In the Bible, it says that we are His own SPECIAL treasure.

"For you are a holy people, who belong to the LORD your God. Of all the people on earth, the LORD your God has chosen you to be his own SPECIAL treasure." Deuteronomy 7:6 NLT

Question #4: What is a treasure? A treasure is something of great worth or value.

Question #5: Do you have any treasures hidden in your room? What are they? Do you watch over (protect) your treasures? Are they SPECIAL to you?

God watches over His treasures, just as mommy and daddy watch over you, and just as you watch over the things you treasure. We protect those things or persons who are SPECIAL to us—just as God does!

ACTIVITY:

- After the lesson, have your children water the same plant as yesterday. Once again, DO NOT water the second plant. Soon we will discover the mystery!

- **Activity for one child**: Let's play *Hot or Cold*. Hide a SPECIAL object from your child such as a special toy, blanket, or a picture of someone special. Let your child begin searching for the object. He will start off "cold" and as he begins to walk around, the farther away he goes, the colder he gets. The closer he gets to the object, the warmer he gets until the object is found. Keep updating how close your child is to the object by saying with excitement "cold," "brrr," "freezing" or "warm," "hot," "you're on fire!" Explain that the treasure you hid is very special to your child, just as we are SPECIAL to God.

- **Activity for multiple children**: The game *Hot or Cold* (explained above) will work if the children will take turns. Or take them outside for a lively game of *Hide and Seek*.

- Remind the child that God is always with us, no matter where we are, even though we can't see Him!

Prayer: *Dear God, Mommy said, I am Your* SPECIAL *treasure. Thank you for making me* SPECIAL, *for loving me and watching over me no matter where I am. Please help me remember that You are always with me. Amen!*

DAY 3

PREP FOR MOM...

Today, we will take a look at Psalm 139:11-12 and how God's light is always shining into the lives of His SPECIAL treasures. Your child is His SPECIAL treasure! Familiarize yourself with the following scriptures:

"If I try to hide in the darkness, the night becomes light around me. For even darkness cannot hide from God; to you the night shines as bright as day. Darkness and light are both alike to you." Psalm 139:11-12 TLB

For younger children: "Then I said to myself, 'Oh, he (God) even sees me in the dark! At night I'm immersed in the light!' It's a fact: darkness isn't dark to you (God); night and day, darkness and light, they're all the same to you (God)." Psalm 139:11-12 The Message

ACTIVITY PROPS AND SUPPLIES:

- The two small plants from yesterday
- A flashlight or candle
- White paper (8½ x11)
- Black marker and crayons

SCRIPT FOR MOM...

Today, we are going to talk about how God's light is always shining into the lives of His SPECIAL treasures. You are His SPECIAL treasure!

> **Question #1:** "If you were a superhero, what would your *super-powers* be?" Have fun with it! Take time to let your children act out their super-powers while they run and fly around. Pretend to be in trouble and let your children come save you.

Tell your child that the Bible says that God is the most important superhero ever! He has super powers! Read Psalm 139:11-12 together:

- **For older children**: "If I try to hide in the darkness, the night becomes light around me. For even darkness cannot hide from God; to you (God) the night shines as bright as day. Darkness and light are both alike to you (God)." TLB

- **For younger children**: "Then I said to myself, 'Oh, he (God) even sees me in the dark! At night I'm immersed in the light!' It's a fact: darkness isn't dark to you (God); night and day, darkness and light, they're all the same to you (God)." The Message

These verses tell us that darkness is not dark to God! He can see everything and everybody—all the time! Remember, He watches over His SPECIAL treasure! We've already learned that:

- God has the power to read our minds.

- He always knows where we are and what we are doing.

- We can never be lost from God because he knows and sees everything!

- Now, we learn that God can see in the dark!

> **Question #2:** Do you remember a time when our electricity went out and the house was dark? Talk to your child about what it felt like to be in the dark.
>
> - Were you afraid?
>
> - Does the dark make you feel anxious?

Take a flashlight into a room with no windows. Hold hands and talk about what it's like for them when it is dark. Then turn on the flashlight and talk about what it is like with the flashlight on. Did having a flashlight or candle make the darkness not seem so dark?

Being in the dark can be frightening. Since we can't see, we don't know what's happening or what to do about it. We feel better about everything in the light, when we can see where we are and what is going on around us. Explain to your child:

- That darkness on the outside is very similar to sadness, anger, or hurt feelings on the inside. It makes us feel yucky!

- The good news is that God loves us so much and He wants to help us because we are SPECIAL to Him.

- Not only does He want to help us not be afraid of the dark, He also wants to help us find our way into the light.

- God wants our hearts to be happy. Even when we feel really bad, God can enter our dark, sad hearts and shine His SPECIAL light to make them happy again. He doesn't even need a flashlight!

Darkness is not dark to God! He can see everything and everybody—all the time! He is always watching over His special treasure!

We are learning so much about how SPECIAL we are to God and how much He loves us and wants to take care of us! Not only does He take care of us on the outside, He also wants to take care of us on the inside! God sure does think we are SPECIAL, doesn't He?

Note: If your children are very young, use this conversation to focus on feelings and plant spiritual seeds for future conversations about salvation. If your children are old enough to understand the concept of salvation, use this conversation to reveal how God, through Jesus's death and resurrection, wants to give us the gift of His Holy Spirit to transform us from the inside out. He wants to get rid of the darkness in our lives (sin) and replace it with his light (salvation).

ACTIVITY:

- Go outside and water the first plant and, once again, DO NOT water the second. What do your children see happening to the plant that gets plenty of water? What do they notice about the one with no water? Our mystery is about to be revealed!

- Fold an 8½ x 11 white sheet of paper in half to make a crease. On one side, have your child draw his facial expression when he is in the dark. On the other side, have him draw his facial expression when the lights come on. Explain that in the Bible Jesus is called the Light of the World. His light is always shining—even in the dark! "His life is the light that shines through the darkness—and the darkness can never extinguish it." John 1:5 TLB

Prayer: *Dear God, Thank you for showing me how SPECIAL I am to you. When I feel those dark feelings inside of me, I will trust You, the Light, to come in and replace them with a happy heart! Amen!*

DAY 4

PREP FOR MOM...

Today, we will take a look at Psalm 139:13-16 and how God made us just who we are—on purpose. We were created by His SPECIAL design. Familiarize yourself with the following scriptures:

"You made my whole being. You formed me in my mother's body. I praise you because you made me in an amazing and wonderful way. What you have done is wonderful. I know this very well. You saw my bones being formed as I took shape in my mother's body. When I was put together there, you saw my body as it was formed. All the days planned for me were written in your book before I was one day old." Psalm 139:13-16 ICB

ACTIVITY PROPS AND SUPPLIES:

- The two small plants from yesterday
- Washable ink pad
- White paper
- Scissors

For biological children:

- Pictures of yourself when you were pregnant with your children
- Ultrasound & newborn pictures of your children

For adopted children:

- Pictures from the biological family, if you have access to them and feel good about using them
- See alternatives below

SCRIPT FOR MOM...

Today, we will talk about how God created each of us by His SPECIAL design.

Start today off telling your children what it was like for you as you carried them in the womb.

- What was it like when you noticed that first little kick?
- Did they get the hiccups?
- If you have multiple children, share with them how one child differed from the other before they were born.

For biological child: Show your children ultrasound pictures of themselves as well as pictures of you pregnant with them. Finally, show them a few pictures of them when they were newborns. Talk about those sweet first weeks of cuddles and sweet kisses.

For an adopted child: Take time to play babies with your little girl. Your little boy may enjoy talking about how long it takes for a momma elephant to have a baby...approximately 22 months! The baby elephant weighs approximately 200 pounds when born! (http://animals.nationalgeographic.com) Elephants are God's unique creation.

Before you were born, God loved you. While He was forming and creating you, He knew how you would fit into His special plan.

Read Psalm 139:13-16 together: "You made my whole being. You formed me in my mother's body. I praise you because you made me in an amazing and wonderful way. What you have done is wonderful. I know this very well. You saw my bones being formed as I took shape in my mother's body. When I was put together there, you saw my body as it was formed. All the days planned for me were written in your book before I was one day old." Psalm 139:13-16 ICB

Explain to your children that even before they were born, God loved them. While He was forming and creating them, He knew how they would fit into His SPECIAL plan.

Help your child understand that no matter whom he is or what he looks like, God made him exactly how He wanted him to be! He is uniquely different and SPECIAL.

Question #1: Do you know what makes snowflakes unique and SPECIAL?

Explain that millions of snowflakes fall every year around the world, and yet no two snowflakes are alike! Every single snowflake is completely unique. That is amazing, isn't it?

Just as amazing is the fact that of all the human beings who have lived, now live, and will live on the earth, God created each one SPECIAL and as a unique creation!

Believe it or not—no one else is just like you. Your physical appearance, your voice and personality traits, your habits, intelligence, personal tastes—all these make you one of a kind.

Question #2: Did you know that your fingerprints separate you from every other human being—past, present, or future? You are unique and your fingerprints are one of a kind!

Ask your children questions that will show them God's specific plan when He created them.

- Do you have curly hair? God made you that way on purpose.
- Do you have dark/tan/light skin? God made you that way on purpose.
- Are you tall? God made you that way on purpose.
- Do you have _____ eyes? God made you that way on purpose.

Why did God make us SPECIAL and unique? Because we "belong to the Lord." Romans 14:8 ICB

For older children: Our design and our uniqueness tell HIS story!! Everybody in the world needs to know who God is and how much He loves them. Some of those people will only understand this very important truth through how you live your life. You, His SPECIAL creation, are a valuable part of helping the whole world know God loves them! You were created ON PURPOSE!

ACTIVITY:
- Go outside and water the first plant, but DO NOT water the second. What do you notice today? Are the plants looking different from each other? Is our mystery becoming clear?

- At the top of each 8½ x 11 sheet of paper write: I am SPECIAL and UNIQUE. Using the washable stamp pad on the white paper, help your child roll each finger on the pad and place their print on the paper. Compare their prints and see how special and unique each one is.

- **For older children**: Go to Pinterest and get instructions on how to cut out snowflakes. See how each is uniquely different.

Prayer: *Dear God, Thank you for making me SPECIAL and unique—just how You wanted me to be. Please help me trust You to take care of me and to teach me Your ways. Amen!*

PREP FOR MOM...

Today, we will take a look at Psalm 139:17-18 and see that God is thinking continually about His SPECIAL creation—you and your child. As His SPECIAL creation, He wants us to tell others about Him. Familiarize yourself with the following scriptures:

"God, your thoughts are precious to me. They are so many! If I could count them, they would be more than all the grains of sand. When I wake up, I am still with you." Psalm 139:17-18 ICB

I love these verses from The Living Bible: "How precious it is, Lord, to realize that you are thinking about me constantly! I can't even count how many times a day your thoughts turn toward me. And when I waken in the morning, you are still thinking of me!" Psalm 139:17-18 TLB

ACTIVITY PROPS AND SUPPLIES:

The two small plants from yesterday

SCRIPT FOR MOM...

Wow! We have learned so much about God this week, haven't we? Can you remember each day's lesson? Let's see if we can say them...

- Day 1: God knows us better than anyone else.
- Day 2: God is watching over us because we are His SPECIAL creation.
- Day 3: God's light is always shining into the lives of His SPECIAL treasures.
- Day 4: God made us just who we are—on purpose. We were created by His SPECIAL design.

Today, we are going to see that God is thinking continually about His SPECIAL creations—us. As His SPECIAL creations, He wants us to tell others about Him.

Question #1: King David wrote Psalm 139 and many other Psalms. In this Psalm, he talks a lot about his favorite thing. Do you know what that was? It was his relationship with God.

Question #2: Talk to your children about some of their favorite things. Ask: Do you think a lot about your favorite things? I am sure you do. Do you tell others about your special things?

We all spend a lot of time thinking about what we love and doing what we love. In fact:

- We spend time singing songs about what we love! That's exactly what King David did!

- King David was a very important king for a people group called Israel.

- King David and the people of Israel lived long, long ago and were chosen by God to be His SPECIAL family.

- God and King David loved each other very much and knew each other very well. God was so SPECIAL to King David that King David wrote songs about Him.

- David was so SPECIAL to God that God chose some of King David's songs to put in the Bible. One of the most special songs was Psalm 139, the Bible verses we have been reading this week!

Question #3: Do you like to sing songs? King David did! God likes it when you sing songs to Him and about Him like King David did. Let's take some time right now to sing about how much God and Jesus love us. (Some suggestions are *Jesus Loves Me*, *Jesus Loves the Little Children*, or let your children make up their own songs about their love for God and Jesus.)

Let's read some of David's song: "How precious it is, Lord, to realize that you are thinking about me constantly! I can't even count how many times a day your thoughts turn toward me. And when I waken in the morning, you are still thinking of me!" Psalm 139:17-18 TLB

These verses help us see how big God's love was for David. God loved David so much that He thought about Him all the time!

God loves us that much, too!! He has so many SPECIAL thoughts about us that they can't even be counted! He put David's song in the Bible so we could read it and always remember God's big giant love for us—His SPECIAL treasure! As His SPECIAL treasure He wants us to tell others about His big giant love for them!

ACTIVITY:

- Now let's discover the mystery of our two plants. Take a look at them. The plant that was watered faithfully this week should look happy and loved. But what does the other plant look like? Is it droopy and sad looking? Has it started turning brown and drying up?

- Lead your children in pretending like they are a flower. A flower starts as a seed (start in a squatting position and cover your head with your arms), then the stem grows tall (still covering your head, stand up slowly), and finally a beautiful flower blooms (uncover your head, stretch out your arms wide, and look up to the sky).

- We have learned this week that just like that little flower needs sunlight and water to grow, God wants to shower us with His love and affection so we will grow and become more like Him. We are loved by God! We are important to God! We are His SPECIAL creation!

- Help your children understand that the flower without water is like someone who has never been told about God or His son, Jesus. They do their best to live life on their own but they are sad and lonely. They do not know that God is there, ready to give them what they need to feel loved. Because we are God's treasured possession, He gives us the very important job of telling others about Him.

- God loved King David with a big love. God loves us with a big love. God loves the world with a big love, too. The world needs to know that, and we get to tell them! "You are to go into all the world and preach the Good News to everyone, everywhere." Mark 16:15 TLB (Great memory verse for kids!)

Prayer: *Dear God, thank you that I am Your SPECIAL creation and for taking care of me like the happy flower. Please help me tell others about You so they can feel Your love, too. Amen!*

Prayer

IS TALKING TO GOD

In this week's *Mommy and Me*, we will be talking about PRAYER. From the time a child can speak, he/she can learn to recite prayers. Once they are older, they can begin to say their own prayers. Children learn by example. They watch and emulate what they hear and see. How are you doing Mommy with your PRAYER life? Are they learning from you?

In Luke 11, one of Jesus' disciples asked him to teach them how to pray. His disciples knew that the habit of His life was PRAYER. His ministry here on earth was rooted in PRAYER

There are a variety of verses in the Bible on PRAYER. The one most quoted contains the words of Jesus in response to the disciple's request to teach them how to pray: "So when you pray, you should pray like this, 'Our Father in heaven, we pray that your name will always be kept holy. We pray that your kingdom will come. We pray that what you want will be done here on earth as it is in heaven. Give us the food we need for each day. Forgive the sins we have done, just as we have forgiven those who did wrong to us. And do not cause us to be tested; but save us from the Evil One.' The kingdom, the power, and the glory are yours forever. Amen." Matthew 6:9-13 ICB

What are you teaching your child about prayer? Jesus set an example for us as to the priority of PRAYER in our lives.

Ready! Set! PRAY!

DAY 1

PREP FOR MOM...

Testimony on PRAYER: "I have always loved to pray. I've always counted it an honor and privilege to be able to talk honestly and candidly with the Lord of the Universe. However, since becoming a mommy, it has taken on a whole new role in my life—that of a lifeline. There are days when PRAYER is the only way I keep my sanity! It's nice to have someone else to talk to besides my 2 and 4 year olds. This *mommying* thing is HARD.

> *There are days when prayer is the only way I keep my sanity! It's nice to have someone else to talk to besides my 2 and 4 year old.*

Mom, have you ever thought about what an amazing reality it is that you get to be in conversation with the Creator of the Universe? You are speaking with the One who "fearfully and wonderfully" made your children.

Familiarize yourself with the following verses:

"For you created my inmost being; you knit me together in my mother's womb. I praise you because I am fearfully and wonderfully made; your works are wonderful, I know that full well. My frame was not hidden from you when I was made in the secret place. When I was woven together in the depths of the earth, your eyes saw my unformed body. All the days ordained for me were written in your book before one of them came to be." Psalm 139:13-16 NIV

"Thus says the Lord, your Redeemer, and the one who formed you from the womb, I, the Lord, am the maker of all things, stretching out the heavens by Myself and spreading out the earth all alone." Isaiah 44:24 NASB

This all powerful, able to create all things, all loving God knows your child in the most perfect way—because He created him exactly how He meant to create him! He did so with purpose—because He has plans for him in His huge Redemptive Story. Therefore, God is THE BEST person to be in conversation with about your child.

Take confidence in this. Go before His throne with courage for He desires to hear you dialogue with Him about your child. He knew his form, structure, personality, and strengths before the beginning of time. And He loves him with His perfect love.

ACTIVITY PROPS AND SUPPLIES:

- Index cards
- Markers
- Decorating materials, i.e. stickers, ribbon, etc.

SCRIPT FOR MOM...

Read: "For you created my inmost being; you knit me together in my mother's womb. I praise you because I am fearfully and wonderfully made; your works are wonderful, I know that full well." Psalm 139:13-14 NIV

Explain: This verse tells us that each of us has been made by God. Each of us was put together exactly how He wanted us to be; and He wanted each of us to be different! All things—everything and every person—that God makes are wonderful—you included!

> **Question #1:** What are some things that you think make you special and wonderful? Allow them time to answer. Then say, "Here are some of the things that I believe are special about you..." (List qualities of your child that you know God created in him.)

Explain: Here is an amazing Truth: You were purposely made unique by the Creator of the Universe with plans to be a part of His Great Redemptive Story. God is doing some amazing things around us, and He created YOU to be a part of those things.

But here is another amazing thing—we get to talk to the God that made you and me!! We get to tell Him things, thank Him for things, and ask Him for things. We get to talk to Him just like you and I are talking right now. There is a word for this conversation that we get to have with our Creator.

> **Question #2:** Do you know what the word is! PRAYER

Read: "Be joyful always; PRAY continually; give thanks in all circumstances, for this is God's will for you in Christ Jesus." I Thessalonians 5:16-17 NIV

This verse tells us that the God who created us wants to hear from us at all times. It makes God happy when we PRAY! He created you—and He likes it when you and I talk to Him.

If your child likes music, the following can be sung to the tune of *Are You Sleeping* to teach them what PRAYER is:

PRAYER is talking, PRAYER is listening

To our God, With our God,

In the morning, In the evening

Anytime, Anywhere

ACTIVITY: *Prayer Cards*

- Write down each of your child's unique qualities on index cards. Write down both his responses as well as yours. Allow him to decorate each card with markers, stickers, etc. Explain to him that you are going to use these cards as your PRAYER/reminder cards while praying for him each day.

- Now take time to PRAY with your child and thank God for making him. Use your newly made PRAYER cards. Don't rush this time! Savor the fact that you are talking to the Almighty Creator about your child in front of that child. After your PRAYER time, let your child know that you, as his mother, are committing to PRAY for him as God reveals His plan for him.

Prayer: *Dear God, thank you for making me special and for making me one of Your own. I am so glad You are always listening for my voice. I want to talk to You every day. Amen!*

DAY 2

PREP FOR MOM...

Testimony on PRAYER: "One night after I had PRAYED for our oldest, Zachary, I asked him if he wanted to pray. He responded yes, and with his precious 4-year-old vocabulary and spirit he sincerely conversed with our Heavenly Father. At the end, like it was the most natural thing in the world, he quoted, "'May the Lord bless you and protect you. May the Lord smile on you and be gracious to you. May the Lord show you his favor and give you his peace. Amen.'" With a lump in my throat, I gave my son the tightest hug I can remember, tucked him into his bed, walked out his door, and came face to face with the reality: Our sons are learning to talk to the Creator of the universe by listening to their father and me! Numbers 6:24-26, is the scripture PRAYER that I pray over our boys every night. It has been a privilege to intercede for them using this verse.

Familiarize yourself with the following verses and truth from a fellow mommy:

"'May the Lord bless you and protect you. May the Lord smile on you and be gracious to you. May the Lord show you his favor and give you his peace." Numbers 6:24-26 NLT

> *It is our responsibility to teach our children about Him, His ways, and how to have a relationship with Him—which includes prayer. Prayer is simply conversing or talking with God.*

It is as simple as that. There is no four-step program, no video series and no website for teaching our children how to PRAY. They are simply listening to us at mealtimes, in the car, at church, before bed, and any other time we choose to PRAY in front to them. "Fix these words of mine in your hearts and minds; tie them as symbols on your hands and bind them on your foreheads. Teach them to your children, talking about them when you sit at home and when you walk along the road, when you lie down and when you get up." Deuteronomy 11:18-19 NIV

- He was telling us as parents that it is our responsibility to TEACH our children about Him, His ways, and how to have a relationship with Him—PRAYER is a part of that.

- The best way to do that is to simply converse with the Lord in front of them—at home and as you walk throughout your day.

- Just like in everything else they watch us do, they'll start to pick up on it—whether we realize it or not!

ACTIVITY PROPS OR SUPPLIES:

- Bean Bags or any item you can use for *tossing*

SCRIPT FOR MOM...

Read: "Fix these words of mine in your hearts and minds; tie them as symbols on your hands and bind them on your foreheads. Teach them to your children, talking about them when you sit at home and when you walk along the road, when you lie down and when you get up." Deuteronomy 11:18-19 NIV

Explain: These were the words God commanded the Israelites after giving them the Ten Commandments. He was telling us, mommies and daddies, that it is our responsibility to TEACH our children about Him, His ways, and how to have a relationship with Him—which includes PRAYER. PRAYER is simply conversing or talking with God.

Question #1: What do you think Mommy is doing when she prays?

Explain: Did you know that God wants to spend time with us? And do you know that one of my favorite things to do when I spend time with you is to talk to you? God is the same way! He wants us to talk to Him.

Question #2: Who is one of your favorite people to talk to? Why? (Relate what he says to God wanting to talk to us—His favorite, i.e. to hear about our day, our dreams, etc.)

Explain: God talks and listens to us just like you would your best friend. One of the most important things we can do with God is talk to Him. Just like with a new friend—that's how we get to know Him. The Bible says, "The Lord would speak to Moses face to face, as a man speaks with his friend." Exodus 33:11. (NIV) God truly cares about what we are feeling, what we want to do, what we are afraid of, and what makes us happy.

The Bible tells us of lots of different times when people prayed. Choose One: Jonah in Jonah 2, Paul and Silas in Acts16:16-34, and Jesus in Matthew 19:13-14.

ACTIVITY: *Prayer Toss*

- Explain to your child that you are going to take turns talking to God. Assure him that God loves to hear from us. It makes Him happy when we talk to Him. You will go first and thank God for something. After you are finished, toss the chosen object to your child, meaning it is his turn to thank God for something. When he is finished, direct him to toss it back to you, indicating that it is your turn again.

- After a few "rounds" of thanking God, tell your child that you are now going to ask God for some things. Encourage him to do the same when it is his turn.

- Depending on your child's age, you may want to allow for rounds for praise, adoration and confession. Remind your child that it doesn't matter where you are or what you are doing, you can always PRAY. Make your PRAYER toss as simple or as elaborate as you would like. Remember God wants us to PRAY with a joyful heart. And having fun with your child can bring a joyful heart!

Prayer: *If you are not already doing so, PRAY, out loud, in the presence of your children. Simply converse with our Heavenly Father in the same way you would if you were alone—adjusting your language only in cases where it may be more understandable to them. End your time today with PRAYING aloud with your children.*

DAY 3

PREP FOR MOM...

Testimony on PRAYER: "I can't explain PRAYER. I don't completely understand God's sovereignty and how my pleadings and requests work into it. But, I do truly believe that my God hears me when I call, no matter how softly or loudly. And I do have faith that He places enormous value on my PRAYERS to Him."

"The Lord detests the sacrifice of the wicked, but the prayer of the upright pleases Him." Proverbs 15:8 NIV

Familiarize yourself with the following verses:

"I love the Lord, for He heard my voice; He heard my cry for mercy. Because He turned His ear to me. I will call on Him as long as I live...Be at rest once more, Oh my soul, for the Lord has been good to you." Psalm 116:1-2,7 NIV

> *I can't explain prayer. I don't completely understand God's sovereignty and how my pleadings and requests work into it. But, I do truly believe that my God hears me when I call, no matter how softly or loudly. And I do have faith that He places enormous value on my prayers to Him.*

"Praise the Lord, all you nations; extol Him, all you peoples. For great is His love toward us, and the faithfulness of the Lord endures forever. Praise the Lord." Psalm 117:1-2 NIV

One of the greatest joys of PRAYER is the assurance that the Lord hears us. Sometimes, He answers our PRAYERS quickly and gives us what we are asking of Him. At other times, He is silent and asks us to wait for an answer. No matter the method, we can trust His perfect timing and divine purpose—He always knows what is best for us. In the process, our faith is strengthened. Faith is the foundation of our relationship with God Almighty—and PRAYER is a major aspect of that foundation.

- Satan strives to convince us that our PRAYERS do not matter.
- The father of lies whispers into our minds that our thanksgiving and petitions are too small and insignificant for God to hear or even care about.

- The enemy desires for our lives to be filled with so many other people, things, and *good works* that our PRAYERS are pushed to the side or simply forgotten.

- He doesn't want us communicating with *El Roi*, the God who sees and hears.

- We must **choose** to believe that our Heavenly Father hears us!

- God not only desires for us to listen to Him but also to talk to Him, to include Him in the conversations of our lives.

ACTIVITY PROPS AND SUPPLIES:

- Construction paper or card stock, white paper or colored copy paper

- Markers, crayons and stickers

- Hole punch, brads or yarn

SCRIPT FOR MOM...

Explain: I have enjoyed talking to you about PRAYER this week! I'm glad we got to learn about this because it's one of the most important things about knowing God.

Question #1: Is it always easy to listen to Mommy?

Question #2: Why is it sometimes hard to listen to Mommy? Possible answers: Sometimes I am distracted, I don't like what you are saying, noises keep me from hearing you or I've heard you say that before so I ignore you. Respond: All of those answers make sense to me. In fact, I've felt that way before when I'm trying to listen to someone. Listening is an important part of PRAYER. His Word says...

Read: "Then you will call upon me and come and PRAY to me, and I *will* listen to you." Jeremiah 29:12 NIV

Explain: God was talking to His children. He is telling them: I will always hear you! The awesome thing about God is that He ALWAYS hears us when we talk to Him. He is never too tired, too busy, or distracted by noises to hear us when we pray. He promises to listen.

Question #3: What do you think God does when we ask Him for something?

Explain: God answers in three possible ways when we ask Him for something: (1) Yes (2) No (3) Wait. His answer is always based on what is best for us. Why? Because He loves us so much, He wants to give us the very best and He has the power to give us the very best. Tell of times when your child asked you for something and the answer was one of the three.

ACTIVITY: *Prayer Journal*

- Recall the ways God has answered your PRAYERS in the past week or month. On paper, list your specific requests and how He answered them. Next, think about how His answers were good and best in the big picture of your personal journey.

- Explain to your child that you are going to keep a record of how God is answering his PRAYERS. Tell him that it is important to always look to see how God is answering our PRAYERS so we can *remember* to thank Him.

- Put together his PRAYER journal using construction paper or cardstock as the cover and white or colored copy paper as the inner pages. Punch holes in the "binder" of the book that can be secured with yarn or brads. Allow your child to decorate the front cover of the journal with markers, crayons and stickers to personalize it. Emphasize that this is his personal journal of how God answered his PRAYERS.

- Time to start journaling. Open to the first page and write the present date. Lead your child to think of things he has asked of God recently or would like to ask of God today. Ask the child to write these on the first page—aiding as much as required for his age. Explain that you and he will look at and add to his journal regularly and when God answers one of his prayers—writing down the specific request along with the date it was answered. Furthermore, explain that he can continue to add requests, reminding him that God loves to hear from us.

- Remember to rejoice with your child when God answers one of his PRAYERS and lead him in thanking our God for always hearing and answering.

Prayer: *Dear God, thank you for hearing and answering our prayers. You are a great God! Amen!*

DAY 4

PREP FOR MOM...

"A wife of noble character who can find? She is worth far more than rubies. Her husband has full confidence in her and lacks nothing of value. She brings him good, not harm, all the days of her life...When it snows she has no fear for her household: for all of them are clothed in scarlet...She watches over the affairs of her household and does not eat the bread of idleness. Her children arise and call her blessed; her husband also, and he praises her." Proverbs 31:10-12, 21, 28-29 NIV

> *The most important thing I can do is pray over my home. I need to be regularly asking our Heavenly Father to protect my house and my family from the Evil One and his destructive plans for our home.*

Testimony of PRAYER: "One of the specific things I remember writing into my wedding vows to my husband was the commitment to do everything possible to make our home a safe haven for him and our future children. For the past several years, I have worked hard at doing that. I've tried to always have a listening ear, be generous with my words of encouragement, and have a favorite meal cooked at the end of a long day. Sometimes, I feel as if I've succeeded, and sometimes, not. But as with so many other realizations that have come with becoming a mommy, it has become clear to me that I must ultimately depend on God to do this. He is the best at creating the *sanctuary* that I so desire for my family. He possesses the power (Psalm 147:5), love (Ephesians 3:18-19), and knowledge of what the true battles are which could bring destruction to our home (Ephesians 6:12).

The most important thing I can do is PRAY over my home. I need to be regularly asking our Heavenly Father to protect my house and my family from the Evil One and his destructive plans for our home. In fact, since coming to this realization, I spend time in the mornings before our children wake up literally walking from room to room asking specific things from our Father, our Protector. As a result, I enter my day with a confidence that our home is protected and ready for whatever our day might hold. And as a mother, that is a wonderful gift. "For God did not give us a spirit of timidity, but a spirit of power, of love and of self-discipline." II Timothy 1:7 NIV

ACTIVITY PROPS AND SUPPLIES:

- Brightly colored paper
- Markers
- Envelopes and a container to place *treasures* in

SCRIPT FOR MOM...

Question #1: Who is your favorite superhero? Why?

Question #2: Do you like them because they protect people? Who do you think protects our house and us while we are in it?

Read: "Unless the Lord builds the house, its builders labor in vain. Unless the Lord watches over the city, the watchmen stand guard in vain." Psalm 127:1 NIV

Explain: This verse tells us that it is God who protects our house. He is the *guard* of our house!

Question #3: What are some of your favorite things about our home? (Reply by telling them some of the things that you are thankful for about your home, i.e. warm beds, air conditioning in the summer, food in the pantry, etc.)

Explain: God is the one who gave us our home and possessions, because He likes to take care of us. Now think of this, not only did God give us our home; but, just like that verse says, He is the one who can protect it best. Mommy (and Daddy) work hard to make our home wonderful, but it is really God who does most of the work.

Read: "Great is our Lord and mighty in power; His understanding has no limits." Psalm 147:5 NIV

Explain: If God is bigger and more powerful than anyone or anything, and the Bible says that He is the best protector of our house, then don't you think it would be smart to talk to Him about this and ask Him to protect our house? God knows that our home is very important and special to us. He knows that it is where our family spends a lot of time. He wants to hear from us about our home and those who live within it. So, if the most powerful God is guarding our house, then we have no reason to be scared.

Question #4: What did we learn about PRAYER yesterday?

ACTIVITY: *Prayer Treasure Hunt*

- Prior to doing this with children, walk around your home in the quietness of the morning, requesting specific things from God that would create a sanctuary within the walls of your house. PRAY scripture as you walk from room to room. Suggested scripture passages: Psalm 33, Galatians 5:22-26, Ephesians 3:14-20 and Ephesians 6:10-18

- Prepare a *treasure* for some of the major rooms of your home (i.e. living room, kitchen, bedrooms, dining room, etc.) Do this by making a list of the things you are thankful for about that room (Ex. warm beds and clothes—bedroom, fun play times—living room, good food—breakfast room.)

- Next list things you would like to ask God for in regard to that room (ex. good rest—bedroom, fun family time—breakfast room, times of learning—play room.) Put these lists on brightly colored paper and place each in its own envelope. Hide the envelopes in the corresponding rooms.

- Lead your child through the house and find the *prayer treasures* in each room. Once each one is found, read the list together. Spend time thanking God for His provisions and making specific requests for each part of your home. Collect the *treasures* in a basket or decorated box/container. Explain to your child that God is the ultimate provider and protector of your home. But as we discussed previously, He loves to be in conversation with us about our lives, and that includes our home.

Prayer: *Dear God, You are more powerful than anything or anyone—thank You for protecting our home. Amen!*

DAY 5

PREP FOR MOM…

Testimony on PRAYER: "From my earliest years of childhood, I remember my parents praying, out loud, each morning for each of their children. They fought for us through intercession to the Most High God. And to this day, even as I am now an adult and parent myself, I know that each morning, they continue to fight for me in this way. Furthermore, I have seen how God has answered their PRAYERS over and over again in my life. So I have chosen to do the same for our sons. Satan might go after them, but they have an earthly mother and father who are doing battle for them under the command of the Most High Commander who has complete power and capability of protecting and leading them."

"No weapon forged against you will prevail, and you will refute every tongue that accuses you. This is the heritage of the servants of the Lord, and this is their vindication from me." Isaiah 54:17 NIV

Acknowledge God's might and ask Him to protect your child and to lead you as you raise and train him up for His Kingdom. Ask Him to cover your child with the Truth of His power and love. Ask God to grow your child "in wisdom, and stature, and in favor with God and men." Luke 2:52 NIV

"Several months ago, we discovered some things about our youngest son's early life (he was adopted into our family at the age of 6 months) that could possibly bring some challenges into his development and journey. It would be easy for the world, and for his parents, to put him in a box and predict how these challenges would affect him. However, we have made the choice to fight for our son in PRAYER, and do whatever it takes to aid him as he grows. Like Hannah, I know that prayer is the most powerful way we can fight for our son."

- Hannah spoke the following words about her son, Samuel. "I prayed for this child, and the Lord has granted me what I asked of Him. So now I give him to the Lord. For his whole life he will be given over to the Lord." I Samuel 1:27-28 NIV

- For years, she prayed that God would grant her a son. And when He did, she committed his life to her Lord's care and direction. She acknowledged that God would ultimately be sovereign over her son's life. Our children are growing up in a world with an enemy who seeks to destroy them. Satan doesn't want them to grow up to be followers of Christ.

- The reality is that our children are his target. But we as parents must believe that "He that is in us is bigger than he that is in the world." God is our children's Jehovah-Nissi, their Banner that goes before them in battle. Claim this truth for your children.

ACTIVITY PROPS AND SUPPLIES:

- Common household items and furniture

SCRIPT FOR MOM...

Question #1: The age of your child will determine how to word this question. What is one of the hardest things for you to do right now? Are you experiencing a hard thing right now? What are you struggling with right now? Respond: I know that has to be hard. But I am so proud of you trying, practicing, enduring, and obeying (whatever the case may be here).

Question #2: Do you know that Mommy loves to help you when things are hard? And do you know one of the best things Mommy can do for you? Answer: PRAY for you!

We've talked about PRAYER this week; do you remember what all we've talked about?

- What PRAYER is: Talking to God.

- God made us and wants to hear from us.

- God always hears and answers our PRAYERS.

- We can ask God to protect our home—and He will.

These are the reasons mommy (daddy) talks to God about you! I know He made you, He loves you, He has the power to protect you, and He wants the very best for you. I also know that hard things sometimes happen to you and around you. And although Mommy (daddy) is always going to do her best to protect you, I know that God is the best protector of you.

Read: "You are my hiding place; You will protect me from trouble and surround me with songs of deliverance." Psalm 32:7 NIV

Explain: The man who wrote this verse, David, had come against some pretty bad stuff and some pretty bad people. But He knew that God was the One who was protecting him. And this entire book (show your child how many Psalms there are) is filled with his PRAYERS of asking God to keep on doing just that—protecting him. Remind your child: Mommy (daddy) prays every day for God to protect you and help you through hard things.

> **Question #3:** Are there any things that you would like Mommy to pray for you about today? Wait and allow the child to think it through. Promise to pray about the concern.

Think about areas you already see Satan attacking or preparing to attack your child. Intercede specifically in these areas. Acknowledge God's might and ask Him to protect your child and to lead you as you raise and train him up for His Kingdom. Ask Him to cover your child with the Truth of His power and love. Ask God to grow your child "in wisdom, and stature, and in favor with God and men." Luke 2:52 NIV

ACTIVITY: *Obstacle Course*

- Inside or outside of your home—create an obstacle course. Do not search for *special* items. Use what you already have, i.e. furniture, beanbags, blankets, etc. Create the course so that he must crawl over, under, and through things. The point is that your child encounters things that will slow him down. Note: The age of your child will dictate the degree of difficulty of the course. Next, have your child go through the course—as many times as he would like.

- Offer to time him if it would be more fun. Go through the course yourself and have a competition with your child on who can complete the course the fastest. Ask: What was the *hardest* part of the course. Explain that there are always going to be things in our lives that are *hard*—things that slow us down. Some will be *experiences*—some will be *people*. Assure the child that these are never a surprise to God and that we can always ask Him to help us. (The correlation works even better if you have had to aid your child with some aspect of the obstacle course.) Remind your child that you will always pray for him when *hard* things happen, knowing that our all powerful God will hear you.

Prayer: *Dear God, thank you for protecting me and helping me through hard things. Amen!*

THE GIFT OF
Forgiveness

In this week's *Mommy and Me*, we will be talking about FORGIVENESS. As parents, we teach FORGIVENESS from a very young age. When a child hits a friend or sibling, after we deal with the punishment, we talk to the child about either asking for FORGIVENESS or granting FORGIVENESS.

FORGIVENESS is the key to moving beyond a hurt or wound that someone has inflicted upon us. Christ set the example for us when it comes to FORGIVENESS. As He was dying on the cross He spoke these words, "Father, forgive them, for they do not know what they are doing." Luke 23:34 (NASB) If, Jesus could forgive those who persecuted Him and hung Him on a cross, we should be able to FORGIVE any offense inflicted upon us.

We will be basing this week's devotional on the following verse: "Be kind to one another, tenderhearted, forgiving one another, as God in Christ forgave you." Ephesians 4:32 ESV

As with all Biblical concepts and truths, children learn from seeing them lived out. So, when it comes to seeing and learning about FORGIVENESS and how to receive and grant FORGIVENESS, they are looking to you—the parent.

> *"Be kind to one another, tenderhearted, forgiving one another, as God in Christ forgave you." Ephesians 4:32 ESV*

Ready! Set! FORGIVE!

DAY 1

PREP FOR MOM...

Today we will be talking about God's FORGIVENESS to us. Familiarize yourself with the following verses:

"If we confess our sins, he is faithful and just to forgive us our sins and to cleanse us from all unrighteousness." 1 John 1:9 ESV

"In Christ we are set free by the blood of his death. And so we have forgiveness of sins because of God's rich grace." Ephesians 1:7 ICB

ACTIVITY PROPS AND SUPPLIES:

- Poster board
- Recipe or large index cards
- Black marker
- Glue stick/Bottle of glue
- Fun easy dessert recipe and ingredients

SCRIPT FOR MOM...

In today's lesson we will be talking about God's FORGIVENESS to us.

> **Question #1:** Do you know what the word FORGIVENESS means? (To grant pardon for, to cancel a debt, to cease to feel resentment for)
>
> **Question #2:** Did you know that the Bible tells us that God will forgive the things we do wrong?

It says, "In Christ we are set free by the blood of his death. And so we have forgiveness of sins because of God's rich grace." Ephesians 1:7 ICB

And another verse says, "If we confess our sins, he is faithful and just to forgive us our sins and to cleanse us from all unrighteousness." 1 John 1:9 ESV

These verses tell us that God will grant us FORGIVENESS for doing wrong, but what must we do first? Confess or admit your wrongdoing.

> *Because of our sin, Christ died FOR us. And, His death grants us forgiveness.*

Your child enjoys hearing stories about when you were growing up. Tell your child a story of a time that you did something very wrong and had to confess to your parents. Talk about the way your parents handled the situation and the FORGIVENESS they granted you.

- Explain the concept of *granting* forgiveness to another person.
- Because *granting* forgiveness may be a difficult concept for a child to understand, you might use the example of a prisoner who's committed a crime.
- Have your child imagine that this person is in prison, but a judge FORGIVES him of his crime and sets that prisoner free.
- In this scenario, the prisoner is still very much guilty.
- His freedom doesn't take away the fact that a crime was committed. BUT…the judge demonstrates kindness, grace and mercy and *grants* FORGIVENESS rather than punishment.

Question #3: Do you remember a time when you did something wrong and had to confess it to mommy (daddy)?

Question #4: How did you feel after you_____? (State the offense mentioned above.) Were you sad, scared that mommy (daddy) would find out?

Question #5: How did you feel after you confessed? How did you feel when mommy (daddy) forgave you?

In our own lives, we all do things wrong (we sin). You may need to help your child understand human mess ups that are SIN: pride, lies, selfishness, stealing, cheating, etc.

Explain: Because of our sin, Christ died FOR us. And, His death grants us FORGIVENESS. We are still guilty of our wrongdoing. But, He chose to pardon us and set us FREE through His FORGIVENESS. We should live lives of gratefulness for our FORGIVENESS.

ACTIVITY: *A Recipe for Forgiveness*

- Across the top of your poster board write this verse from today's lesson: "If we confess our sins, he is faithful and just to forgive us our sins and to cleanse us from all unrighteousness." 1 John 1:9 ESV

- Ask: If we were to create a recipe for forgiveness, what ingredients would you need? You may want to prompt the child's thinking with words such as: grace, mercy, love, etc.

- Using the recipe cards (large index cards) write each response in bold lettering on a card.

- Glue the cards on your poster board and place it in a prominent place while teaching this week's devotional on FORGIVENESS.

- Allow the child to prepare a recipe for a fun dessert with you. As you eat the treat you have prepared, talk about how grateful we should be for God's FORGIVENESS and how He has set an example for us.

Prayer: *Dear God, thank you for FORGIVENESS. I know that I sin, and I need Your FORGIVENESS every day. Help me to receive it and trust YOU. Help me make good choices that honor who YOU are. Amen!*

DAY 2

PREP FOR MOM...

Yesterday, we talked about God's FORGIVENESS to us. Today we will be talking about receiving FORGIVENESS from others.

Read and familiarize yourself with the verse below and the story of the Lost or Prodigal Son in Luke 15:11-32.

"To him all the prophets bear witness that everyone who believes in him receives forgiveness of sins through his name." Acts 10:43 ESV

ACTIVITY PROPS AND SUPPLIES:

- Beautifully wrapped gift box

SCRIPT FOR MOM...

Remind the child that yesterday, we talked about God's FORGIVENESS to us. Tell him that today we will be talking about receiving FORGIVENESS from others.

> **Question #1:** When we receive something from someone, what do we do? We take possession of it. We acquire it. We take it for our own.
>
> Today we are going to read a story of a young man who ran away from home. The Bible does not give us his name; it only calls him the Lost Son.
>
> **Question #2:** What does it mean when we say something is lost? Relate a story of a time the child or a family member lost something, i.e. a toy, dog, etc.

If the child has ever been lost or lost something have him describe how he felt. If you have ever thought you lost a child in a store or mall, tell how you felt.

Let's read about this lost young man. Note: There are 3 options for reading this story. Choose the one most suited to the age of your child. 1) Use a Children's Bible storybook. 2) Use a translation relatable to the age of your child, i.e. International Children's Bible. 3) You read the story ahead of time and then in summary form tell the story to your child.

If your child is familiar with the story of the Lost Son, you may ask him to retell the story.

Question #3: Why did the son run away and where did he go?

Question #4: Do you remember the part of the story where the son returned home and received his father's FORGIVENESS?

Talk about what it must have been like for the father to see his son in the distance coming home. Relate a time when you were apart from your child and how you felt to see him again.

Question #5: What was his life like before he chose to receive his father's FORGIVENESS? Choosing NOT to receive God's forgiveness keeps us from running to God, our Father. The Lost Son had to return to his father in order to fully receive his FORGIVENESS.

ACTIVITY: *The Gift of Forgiveness*

- Offer your child a beautifully wrapped gift box. (There can be a small gift or piece of candy inside or it can be empty.)

- Ask your child what he would like to do with the gift box. The natural answer would be, "Open it."

- Ask if he would even consider putting the wrapped gift to the side and never opening it.

- Explain that God's FORGIVENESS to us is a gift. We have to accept it. Just like putting that beautifully wrapped present to the side and refusing to open it would be silly, it's just as silly for us to choose to hold on to the guilt of our sin or our wrongdoing instead of receiving God's FORGIVENESS.

- Consider praying over your child's heart today. Cry out to the Father (with your child) asking Him to protect your son or your daughter from Satan's evil snare. He wants to trick us into believing we've gone too far… that we're just too lost to be saved. Right now, pray that God would strengthen your child's heart in HIM, so that Satan's ploys (now and in the future) for your children backfire. Pray that your children have such TRUST in God that they never doubt HIS forgiving power over them.

Prayer: *Dear God, thank you for forgiving me of my sins. I receive your mercy, grace and forgiveness. Thank you for being my Heavenly Father. Amen!*

Day 3

Prep for Mom...

We have talked about God's FORGIVENESS to us, our receiving His FORGIVENESS and today, we will talk about what the Bible says about FORGIVING others outside our family, i.e. friends, schoolmates, teachers, etc..

Familiarize yourself with the following verses:

"Be kind to one another, tenderhearted, forgiving one another, as God in Christ forgave you." Ephesians 4:32 ESV

"Yes, if you forgive others for the things they do wrong, then your Father in heaven will also forgive you for the things you do wrong. But if you don't forgive the wrongs of others, then your Father in heaven will not forgive the wrong things you do." Matthew 6:14-15 ICB

Activity Props and Supplies:

- White paper 8 ½ x 11 for coloring
- Crayons or markers
- Pencil or pen

Script for Mom...

Yesterday's lesson on receiving FORGIVENESS was deep. Take some time as you begin today's devotion to check in with your child. Ask for questions and attempt to fill in the blanks where he has questions. Remember, if you don't know the answer, it's ok to say that. Stop and pray over any confusion your child may have.

Explain that today you are going to be talking about showing FORGIVENESS to others. Because God forgives us and we accept His FORGIVENESS, it is then easier for us to forgive others.

Remind your child of the pretend story of the prisoner being pardoned in Day 1. That prisoner was you, and God chose to forgive you. Therefore, He wants us to give the same FORGIVENESS to others that we have been given.

> **Question #1:** Can you recall a time when someone wronged or hurt you? Tell me about it. On an 8½ x 11 white paper, make a written list. No matter what your child considers to be a "wrong," acknowledge its importance. Add it to the list and discuss.
>
> **Question #2:** How did you feel when you were wronged?

If you can, think of a time recently that someone has hurt you. You will probably want to choose a smaller hurt—nothing too heavy for your children to understand. Explain what the hurt was and why it hurt so badly. Dialogue some with your child with the following questions:

- Who is guilty in that story?
- What sin did they commit? Why was it wrong?
- How do you think I wanted to respond?
- How would God want me to respond?

Read the following verses:

"Be kind to one another, tenderhearted, forgiving one another, as God in Christ forgave you." Ephesians 4:32 ESV

"Yes, if you forgive others for the things they do wrong, then your Father in heaven will also forgive you for the things you do wrong. But if you don't forgive the wrongs of others, then your Father in heaven will not forgive the wrong things you do." Matthew 6:14-15 ICB

Talk with your child about these verses and their meaning. Explain that we are not to withhold or hold back our FORGIVENESS. God freely forgives us, and we are to freely forgive others.

> **Question #3:** When we refuse to forgive someone for hurting us or doing wrong to us, who does it hurt? It hurts us, doesn't it? Talk about the ways it can hurt or bring harm to the one refusing to forgive.

Sometimes, it is hard to forgive someone who has hurt us badly. But, holding on to that hurt will continue to cause pain for us because we are going against what God has told us to do— forgive because He has forgiven you.

ACTIVITY: *A Different World*

- Write a list of ways the world (or your home) would be different if more people would forgive one another. Discuss these with your child.

- Fold your 8½ x 11 sheet in half. Open it up. The fold will divide the sheet in half. Have your child color a picture on one side of a time when he was wronged or hurt by someone. On the other side, have him draw a picture of what the relationship would look like after he has forgiven the person who hurt him.

> *We are not to withhold or hold back our forgiveness. God freely forgives us and we are to freely forgive others.*

- Ask your child to look back at the list of wrongs committed against him. Choose one incident from the list and pray with your child about that relationship. Allow your child some time to form a few statements of prayer to God asking for help in forgiving the friend or family member. Then, pray FOR your child and this hurt he has experienced.

Prayer: *Dear God, Your Word tells me that because You have* FORGIVEN *me, I am to forgive* _____ *for* _____. *(Fill in name of the offender and the offense.) I am choosing to forgive and love* _____ *because You have asked me to do so. Amen!*

DAY 4

PREP FOR MOM...

Well, so far this week we have talked about God's FORGIVENESS to us, our receiving His FORGIVENESS and FORGIVING others outside our family, i.e. friends, schoolmates, teachers, etc. Today we will see what the Bible says about forgiving those closest to us, i.e. siblings, mommy, daddy, cousins, aunts, uncles, etc.

Familiarize yourself with the following verses:

> *"Try to understand other people. Forgive each other. If you have something against someone, forgive him. That is the way the Lord forgave you."*
> *Colossians 3:13 NLV*

"Do not hurt someone who has hurt you. Do not keep on hating the sons of your people, but love your neighbor as yourself. I am the Lord." Leviticus 19:18 NLV

"Try to understand other people. Forgive each other. If you have something against someone, forgive him. That is the way the Lord forgave you." Colossians 3:13 NLV

"You must be kind to each other. Think of the other person. Forgive other people just as God forgave you because of Christ's death on the cross." Ephesians 4:32 NLV

ACTIVITY PROPS AND SUPPLIES:

Ingredients for S'Mores:

- Graham crackers
- Hershey milk chocolate bars
- Large marshmallows

SCRIPT FOR MOM...

Explain that so far this week you have talked about God's FORGIVENESS to us, our receiving His FORGIVENESS and FORGIVING others outside our family, i.e. friends, schoolmates, teachers, etc. Today you will see what the Bible says about forgiving those closest to us, i.e. siblings, mommy, daddy, cousins, aunts, uncles, etc.

"Do not hurt someone who has hurt you. Do not keep on hating the sons of your people, but love your neighbor as yourself. I am the Lord." Leviticus 19:18 NLV

> **Question #1:** According to this verse, are we to seek revenge or try to get someone back if they have wronged or hurt us? No! If your brother hits you, are you to hit him back? If your cousin makes fun of you, are you to make fun of him? No!

Yesterday, we talked about forgiving those outside our family who hurt us. Why do we forgive them? Because, God has forgiven us.

> **Question #2:** Do you think it is easier to forgive your friends than it is to forgive your sister/brother? Why is this?

We should forgive those closest to us as easily and quickly as we forgive those outside our family. Why, because God has forgiven us. We are to follow His example!

Read the following verse:

"Try to understand other people. Forgive each other. If you have something against someone, forgive him. That is the way the Lord forgave you." Colossians 3:13 NLV

This verse tells us to try to understand and accept other people, especially those within our family. You are uniquely different because God made you unique and special. As family, we need to accept and try to understand that we are each unique and special.

God tells us that if we are upset, mad, or angry with one another that we should forgive each other.

In the Bible, there are many verses on FORGIVENESS. God is very serious about us forgiving those within our home. Once we forgive those within our family, we are better able to love them and show them kindness.

"You must be kind to each other. Think of the other person. Forgive other people just as God forgave you because of Christ's death on the cross." Ephesians 4:32 NLV

Question #3: What do you think this verse means when it says to "think of the other person?"

Question #4: How would our home be different if each of us was to think of the other person before himself, show kindness and love, and forgive quickly without holding a grudge?

Discuss what a difference this would make in the atmosphere of your home.

God's Word is very clear.... We are to forgive those who hurt us, especially those within our family. Choosing NOT to do so is sin against the Lord, and it is harmful to us.

ACTIVITY:

- Gather all the ingredients for making S'Mores.

- Explain that for the past two days you have talked about forgiving those who have hurt or wronged them—those outside our family and within our family.

- We are not to withhold forgiveness. God has told us that we are to forgive and forgive S'More.

- So, today we are going to make S'Mores, and as we do I want you to remember to forgive S'More and S'More and S'More. When we do it will bring a smile to God's face, just as this treat will bring a smile to your face.

- Allow the children to put their S'Mores together and, if old enough, roast them over the grill or burner—with your assistance, of course!

- Pray with your child asking God for the ability to forgive well. Acknowledge how difficult that can be and thank God that He always makes a way for us to do the hard things when we trust Him. Proverbs 3: 5-6 would be a good verse to pray with your child.

Prayer: *Dear God, thank you for loving me and* FORGIVING *me every time I do something wrong. Help me to forgive anyone who hurts me. Amen!*

DAY 5

PREP FOR MOM...

So far this week we have talked about God's FORGIVENESS to us, our receiving His FORGIVENESS and FORGIVING those within and outside our family.

Today, we will take a look at the Samaritan woman at the well and how Jesus forgave her sins. When He did, she was changed, and everyone could see the change on her face.

Familiarize yourself with the following verses:

Read John 4:5-30, 39-42

One of the verses we have read this week is: "Be kind to one another, tenderhearted, forgiving one another, as God in Christ forgave you." Ephesians 4:32 ESV

If your child is young, be prepared to summarize the story for him. If your child is older, you may want to read the story directly from the Bible.

ACTIVITY PROPS AND SUPPLIES:

- A Mirror
- Construction paper—variety of colors
- Markers

SCRIPT FOR MOM...

> **Question #1:** What have we been talking about the past few days? FORGIVENESS
>
> **Question #2:** What have we learned about FORGIVENESS?

We have learned about God's FORGIVENESS to us and that we have to receive His FORGIVENESS. Then we learned about how important it is to FORGIVE others outside our family and those within our family.

One of the verses we have read this week is: "Be kind to one another, tenderhearted, forgiving one another, as God in Christ forgave you." Ephesians 4:32 ESV

> **Question #3:** So, why do we forgive others? We forgive because God forgives us.
>
> **Question #4:** How do you feel when you have been forgiven for a hurt you inflicted on someone else? You feel good, don't you? Being forgiven changes you. It takes away the sadness of having hurt someone else.
>
> **Question #5:** How do you feel when you have forgiven someone who has hurt you?

We are different when we receive forgiveness from someone we have hurt. We are different when we forgive those who have hurt us. It makes us happy when we forgive and are forgiven, doesn't it!

It brings a smile to our face and to God's!

Mommy wants to tell you a story today about a woman in the Bible.

- We do not know much about her. In fact, we do not even know her name. We do know that she was from a country called Samaria. Can you say that? SAMARIA.

- Jesus met her at Jacob's well as He was traveling. It was a hot day. He was tired and thirsty, so He sat down by the well.

- She came to draw water from the well. Jesus said to her, "Please give me a drink?" This surprised the woman because Jesus was a Jewish man and she was a Samaritan woman—the Jews did not have anything to do with Samaritans.

- Jesus began to tell the woman things about herself—about her life and the way she was living. She was not living for God.

- He told her that He would forgive her for her sins and make her life happy again.

- Jesus forgave her and freed her from her sin. Her meeting with Jesus at the well changed her. She had received FORGIVENESS.

- She ran back to her town and told many others about her encounter with Jesus and how she had been FORGIVEN. Because of her testimony of what Jesus did for her, many of the people in her town became Christians—accepting Jesus as their Savior.

In Matthew 28:19-20, it says, "So go and make followers of all people in the world. Baptize them in the name of the Father and the Son and the Holy Spirit. Teach them to obey everything that I have told you. You can be sure that I will be with you always. I will continue with you until the end of the world." ICB

Explain to your child that these verses were spoken by Jesus to His disciples. They were instructions for them to go and tell others what God had done for them. We, like the disciples and the Woman at the Well, are to go and tell. The Woman at the Well was able to go and tell (spread the Gospel) because she was FORGIVEN—and others noticed!

If we are people who forgive like God does, others will see it. Our ability to forgive will be a reflection of God's forgiveness to others.

> *Clara Barton, the founder of the American Red Cross, was reminded one day of a vicious deed someone had done to her years before. But she acted as if she had never heard of the incident. "Don't you remember it?" Her friend asked. "No." ...came Barton's reply. "I distinctly remember forgetting it." Clara Barton*

ACTIVITY:

- Using a mirror, hold it in front of your child's face. Ask him to remember a time when he was hurt or wounded by someone. Notice the sad face. Now, ask him to remember how he felt when he forgave the one who hurt him. Notice the happy face when he remembers how good it felt to forgive. Reverse the illustration—your child inflicted the hurt and was forgiven by the hurt person—notice the facial difference.

- Make heart shaped cards and write *Please Forgive Me* on the front. The child can use them the next time he hurts or wounds someone close to him. On the back write one of this week's verses.

- Here is a saying your child can memorize: A heart is easily hurt by unkind words we say or even being mean when we play. If you have hurt another, this is what to do—say "I am sorry, forgive me as Jesus forgave me and you."

Prayer: *Dear God, help me to always forgive and to tell others of Your* FORGIVENESS. *Amen!*

GUARD YOUR
Mind

In this week's *Mommy and Me,* we will be talking about our MIND and the THOUGHTS we entertain. Our MIND controls much of what we do, say and think. When our MIND is left unguarded, we can do, say, and think things that are unkind and unpleasing to God.

The following verse from Philippians 4:8 is our launching point this week, "Finally brothers, whatever is true, whatever is honorable, whatever is just, whatever is pure, whatever is lovely, whatever is commendable, if there is any excellence, if there is anything worthy of praise, think about these things." ESV

> *"Finally brothers, whatever is true, whatever is honorable, whatever is just, whatever is pure, whatever is lovely, whatever is commendable, if there is any excellence, if there is anything worthy of praise, think about these things."*
> *Philippians 4:8 ESV*

Guarding our MINDS takes self-discipline. What we want to teach the children this week is how to recognize bad or harmful thoughts and then what to do with those thoughts—how we go about "guarding" our MINDS.

Ready! Set! Guard your MIND!

Day 1

Prep for Mom...

For fun, read a few details about the human brain (the mind). If possible have a picture of the brain:

- The human brain weighs 3.0 pounds and is 60% fat, making it one of the fattiest organs in the body.
- The brain takes the longest of any organ to develop and goes through the most changes of any other organ.
- A human brain is 75% water and has the consistency of gelatin. (Jell-O)
- While awake the brain can generate enough energy to power a light bulb (Between 10-25 watts).
- The human brain has around 100,000 miles of blood vessels. (About the same distance from New York City to Sydney, Australia)
- Approximately 20% of the total oxygen in the human body is used by the brain.
- The brain is the central organ of thought.
- Every thought, feeling and plan we have is developed by the human brain.

Familiarize yourself with the following verse:

"Finally brothers, whatever is true, whatever is honorable, whatever is just, whatever is pure, whatever is lovely, whatever is commendable, if there is any excellence, if there is anything worthy of praise, think about these things." Philippians 4:8 ESV

This week we will be talking about our MIND and the THOUGHTS that we have each and every day: good thoughts, bad thoughts, true thoughts, false thoughts, critical thoughts, mean thoughts, hurtful thoughts, etc.

ACTIVITY PROPS AND SUPPLIES:

- Paper
- Black marker and crayons

SCRIPT FOR MOM...

Today we will be talking about our MINDS and the THOUGHTS we have.

Question #1: Do you know where your brain is? That is right. It is in your head.

Ask the children what they know about the human brain/MIND. Give some of the facts on the human brain listed in this week's Prep for Mom. Explain that our thoughts originate in the brain/MIND. Note: These facts would be best suited for children age 5 and above. If your children are younger, explain that the human brain is an organ of the body (like the heart, lungs etc.) and that the thoughts we have start in our brain/MIND.

Show a picture of the human brain and explain that God created us with a brain/MIND. Our thoughts come from our brains. God wants our thoughts to be pleasing to Him and others.

Read: "Finally brothers, whatever is true, whatever is honorable, whatever is just, whatever is pure, whatever is lovely, whatever is commendable, if there is any excellence, if there is anything worthy of praise, *think* about these things." Philippians 4:8 ESV

Discuss what the different words mean in a way that your children can understand. According to this verse, the thoughts coming from our MINDS are to be true, honorable (deserving of respect), just (reasonable, proper), pure (spotless), lovely (loveable, grand), commendable (praise) and excellent (superior, first-class).

Question #2: What does the word TRUE mean? It means *honest* or *truthful*. If something if TRUE it can be trusted—it is honest.

Question #3: When mommy and daddy ask you to tell the truth, what are we asking of you? We are asking you to be honest with us.

ACTIVITY:

- Play a whisper game of TRUTH and non-TRUTH with your children. See if they recognize the sentences that are untruthful.

- Start with something sweet and true, such as "Jane has beautiful blue eyes." or "God made the earth so beautiful." Whisper the sweet and truthful line into the first child's ear; ask him to whisper it into the next child's ear. Keep going with several little lines that are true and kind. Let them whisper the lines to one another until it makes it back to you.

- Next, intersperse the true lines with something silly and funny, but *false* such as "The moon is upstairs in your bedroom." or "A huge lion is sitting on the porch." Laugh with them as they find humor in the ridiculous. Ask them if these are true. Explain that they are silly, funny and untruthful.

- Then intersperse something that is not true or funny such as "It is great when we hit people." or "The Bible isn't true." Your children may think you are joking but make sure that they see how serious you are at this point. Once the untrue statement has gone all the way around ask them "Is this true?" Note: With one child, you can whisper back and forth. When he whispers the words back, ask him, "is that true?"

- Discuss how the different words made them feel. Talk with them about the importance of listening to things that are true. Bring up the silly lines and discuss how easy it is to laugh at funny things. Explain that it's not bad to be silly sometimes or to use our imaginations, but we need to learn how to recognize what is true and false. Sometimes it can get confusing, especially when it makes us laugh. That's why we can look to God's Word to help us know what to think and talk about.

Draw a picture of them with an exaggerated head and explain that their minds are one of the most powerful parts of their bodies. Let them color objects around their MIND that signify things that are good and lovely and TRUE to think on.

Prayer: *Dear God, guard my* MIND *and help me to think about things that are true and pleasing to You. Amen!*

DAY 2

PREP FOR MOM...

Yesterday we talked about our brains/MINDS and having THOUGHTS that are TRUE. Today we will be talking about how to know when a thought is true or false.

Familiarize yourself with the following verses:

"For the word of God is alive and powerful. It is sharper than the sharpest two-edged sword, cutting between soul and spirit, between joint and marrow. It exposes our innermost thoughts and desires." Hebrews 4:12 NLT

"We capture every thought and make it give up and obey Christ." 2 Corinthians 10:5b ICB

It is important for the children to understand that God is the God of all truth. His Word is alive, powerful and true. When we read the Bible, God's Word, it reveals things to us about ourselves. In Hebrews 4:12, it says God's Word exposes (makes known) our thoughts. God knows what we are thinking at all times and if what we are thinking is true or false. Be prepared to explain the meaning of the word: false. (Not true, to deceive or mislead)

For the verse in 2 Corinthians 10:5b, the children will play a little game of *Capture the Thought*.

ACTIVITY PROPS AND SUPPLIES:

- Rope or twine
- Flour and beans
- Sieve or strainer

SCRIPT FOR MOM...

Question #1: How can we know what is true? (Question may be best for ages 5 and above) If your child is younger, explain how to know when something is true or false. Remind them of the Whisper Game from yesterday and how some things you said were true, some were silly and false, and others were totally false.

God and His Word can help us know what is true and what is false. In the Bible it says, "For the word of God is alive and powerful. It is sharper than the sharpest two-edged sword, cutting between soul and spirit, between joint and marrow. It exposes our innermost thoughts and desires." Hebrews 4:12 NLT

Talk with your children about the Bible being God's *guide book* for us. In His *guide book*, He reveals His character (qualities, traits and who He is) and His absolute truth through the Scripture. Explain to them that the Bible was written by holy men who were inspired (influenced) by God. We can trust the words of the Bible because God Himself is truth. The Bible will help us know what is true and good to think, and also what is false.

> *"We capture every thought and make it give up and obey Christ."*
> 2 Corinthians 10:5b ICB

ACTIVITY #1:

- Explain that false is the opposite of true. Use a sentence or two from your game yesterday as an example.

- To illustrate how we can separate our true thoughts from our false thoughts, do the following exercise: Mix some flour with large dried beans or noodles. Use a sieve or strainer and let your children pour the mixture through. Explain that we want to train our MINDS to be like a sieve that allows what is true and good to come through our thoughts, but keeps out what is false. In order to do this, we need to know the Bible!

- When a false or untrue thought enters our MINDS, the Bible tells us what to do with that thought. It says, "We capture every thought and make it give up and obey Christ." 2 Corinthians 10:5b ICB

ACTIVITY #2:

> **Question #2:** "What does it mean to take someone captive?" It means that you hold onto that person, right?

- Use the rope or twine to capture one of the children. Lightly wrap him in the rope or twine but make sure their arms are secured by his side.

Question #3: Ask the child if he can move his arms? No, because they are held captive by the rope. Note: If you have small children, to illustrate being held captive, hold the child tightly in your lap so he cannot move.

- Explain that when we take our thoughts captive, we hold thoughts prisoner that aren't true or good.

- Instead of allowing them to go free in our MIND, we discover what the Bible has to say and *make* those thoughts obedient to Christ.

- Give an example such as this. When we see someone and think, "That girl is not very good. She's not pretty or special." We can hold that thought captive, tie it up like we did with the rope. We tell ourselves, "Wait!!! God's Word says that each person is fearfully and wonderfully made. She is very special! God made her just the way He wants her!" We took the false thought captive and made it obedient to Jesus and His Word.

For older children: Encourage your children to continue to study the Bible and memorize verses so that they can know truth and take every thought captive to make it obedient to Jesus! Find creative ways to help them get started.

For younger children: Begin to teach them simple short verses from God's Word. A child as young as two can begin to memorize short scripture verses. Use songs as a way of teaching these Biblical truths.

Prayer: *Dear God, thank you that Your Word is true and that it helps me to know when my thoughts are true or false. When a false thought comes into my mind, help me to wrap it up so it cannot hurt me or anyone else. Amen!*

DAY 3

PREP FOR MOM...

Today we are going to use several verses in discussing the remainder of thoughts described in Philippians 4:8.

Familiarize yourself with the following verses:

"Finally brothers, whatever is true, whatever is honorable, whatever is just, whatever is pure, whatever is lovely, whatever is commendable, if there is any excellence, if there is anything worthy of praise, *think* about these things." Philippians 4:8 ESV

"If your sinful old self is the boss over your mind, it leads to death. But if the Holy Spirit is the boss over your mind, it leads to life and peace." Romans 8:6 NLV

> *Our thoughts are to be respectful of others, proper, nice, loving, kind and first class.*

"Out of the mind come evil thoughts...lying, and saying bad things against other people." Matthew 15:19a ICB

"Let the Spirit renew your thoughts and attitudes." Ephesians 4:23 NLT

"I will sing to the Lord as long as I live, I will praise my God to my last breath! May all my thoughts be pleasing to Him, for I rejoice in the Lord." Psalm 104:33-34 NLT

ACTIVITY PROPS AND SUPPLIES:

- White paper
- Black marker
- Lunch sack
- Set of index cards

SCRIPT FOR MOM...

We have talked about thoughts that are true versus thoughts that are false. Today we are going to look at the remaining words in Philippians 4:8 that describe our thoughts: honorable (deserving of respect), just (reasonable, proper), pure (spotless), lovely (lovable, grand), commendable (praise) and excellent (superior, first-class).

- Explain that our thoughts are to be respectful of others, proper, nice, loving, kind and first class.

- When we express thoughts that are kind and loving, they will please God, daddy and mommy, and make others happy—rather than sad.

- Have the children help you make a list of respectful, proper, nice, kind and first-class words. Example: I think Sally is *pretty* or I *like* my teacher and she is *very nice* to me. Talk about *kind* versus *mean* thoughts that we express with our words and how mean, harsh, and untrue words can hurt those around us.

Read: "Out of the mind come evil thoughts…lying, and saying bad things against other people." Matthew 15:19a ICB

So, out of our MINDS can come good thoughts or evil and bad thoughts.

Our thoughts come from our MIND, but the Bible tells us that they really originate (start) in our heart. A bad heart=bad thoughts.

Read: "If your sinful old self is the boss over your mind, it leads to death. But if the Holy Spirit is the boss over your mind, it leads to life and peace." Romans 8:6 NLV

Explain the above verse. You might use your husband's job (or your own) and the role that his (your) boss plays as an illustration of the "control" this verse is speaking of.

Jesus wants to be our "boss." He wants to live in our hearts and have "control" over our thoughts (MINDS). When He lives in our hearts, our thoughts will reflect Him. God is good, loving and kind. So, a Good heart=Good thoughts.

"Let the Spirit (the Holy Spirit) renew (make new/change) your thoughts and attitudes." Ephesians 4:23 NLT

We have learned that we are to take our false thoughts captive, and tie them up with a rope.

When Jesus lives in our hearts, we have a good heart which means a good MIND that will express respectful, good, kind, and loving thoughts.

ACTIVITY:

- Using your list of respectful, proper, nice, kind and first-class words, write each word on an index card.

- Place the cards in a brown paper lunch sack. (Any container will do.)

- During your family dinner time, pull out a card from the bag and go around the dinner table having each member of your family say something nice about the person to their right, until all the cards have been used.

Lead your family in memorizing this verse: "I will sing to the Lord as long as I live, I will praise my God to my last breath! May all my thoughts be pleasing to Him, for I rejoice in the Lord." Psalm 104:33-34 NLT **For younger children:** "I will sing to God and praise Him. I want my thoughts to make Him happy."

Prayer: *Dear God, help my thoughts to be respectful of others, proper, nice, loving, kind and first class. Thank you for being the boss of my* MIND *and thoughts. Amen!*

DAY 4

PREP FOR MOM...

Yesterday, we focused on the other types of thoughts described in Philippians 4:8, which tell us that we are to think respectful, proper, nice, loving, kind and first class thoughts. The children were told that when Jesus is the "boss" of their hearts and MINDS, their thoughts will please Him. He wants us to take captive (tie them up) all thoughts that are false. He wants to control our hearts and MINDS (thoughts). ESV

Today, we want to talk about the times when we have bad thoughts or when others (friends, teachers, etc.) tell us things that cause us to think things we should not—like Satan did with Eve in the Garden.

Familiarize yourself with the following verses:

"Now the snake was the most clever (crafty, sneaky, smart) of all the wild animals the Lord God had made. One day the snake spoke to the woman. He said, "Did God really say that you must not eat fruit from any tree in the garden? The woman answered the snake, "We may eat fruit from the trees in the garden. But God told us, 'You must not eat fruit from the tree that is in the middle of the garden. You must not even touch it, or you will die. But the snake said to the woman, 'You will not die. God knows that if you eat the fruit from that tree, you will learn about good and evil. Then you will be like God!' The woman saw that the tree was beautiful. She saw that its fruit was good to eat and that it would make her wise. So she took some of its fruit and ate it. She also gave some of the fruit to her husband who was with her, and he ate it." Genesis 3:1-6 ICB

"Obey my commands, and you will live. Protect my teachings as you would your own eyes. Remind yourself of them. Write them down in your mind as if on a tablet." Proverbs 7:2-3 ICB

ACTIVITY PROPS AND SUPPLIES:

- Costumes to act out Genesis 3:1-6 (Mommy or Daddy play the part of Satan)
- A small coloring tablet for each child, spiral index cards or journal (depending on the age of each child)
- Black marker
- Colored markers

SCRIPT FOR MOM...

Today, we want to talk about the times when we have bad thoughts or when others (friends, teachers, etc.) tell us things that cause us to think things we should not—like Satan did with Eve in the Garden.

Summarize Genesis 3:1-6. Explain that at one time, Satan had been a glorious angel. But in pride, he rebelled against God (turned away from God) and was thrown out of heaven. He came to the garden disguised as a serpent (pretending to be a snake). He wanted to deceive Eve (lie to her).

Question #1: Whose voice was Eve listening to when she ate of the fruit? God's voice (His Word) or Satan's? Yes, Satan's voice.

God asked Eve why she ate of the forbidden tree. (Explain the word *forbidden*.) She answered, "The serpent (snake) lied to me and said it was okay if I ate from that tree and I believed him." (Genesis 3:13 ICB) Instead of believing truth— what God had said—she believed a lie.

There are 10 Commandments (rules) given in the Bible. The 9th commandment says, "Thou shall not lie." We are not to deceive others (lie to them) as Satan did Eve. God says, "Obey my commands, and you will live. Protect my teachings (God's Word) as you would your own eyes. Remind yourself of them (scriptures/God's Word). Write them down in your mind as if on a tablet." Proverbs 7:2-3 ICB

Mommy and daddy have rules to protect you—Example: You cannot play in the street or you have to hold our hand when we are in a parking lot. God has rules or commandments to protect us and one of them is that we are not to lie.

Sometimes our friends or brothers and sisters will lie to us. Sometimes we are tempted to lie to others.

> **Question #2:** Who tempts us to lie? Satan. When we are tempted, we need to remember that God is a God of truth and He wants us to be truthful.
>
> **Question #3:** Has there ever been a time when you believed a lie that someone told you? What happened?

God put Adam and Eve out of the Garden because they believed Satan's lie.

> **Question #4:** When you have lied to mommy and daddy and we found out about it, what happened? You were punished, weren't you? Lying leads to punishment. Your lie hurts others, like mommy and daddy, your siblings, and the one you lied to or about. Most of all it hurts God's heart. We are never punished for telling the truth and it never hurts us or others— it always makes us feel good and brings a smile to God's face!

ACTIVITY:

- **For younger children:** Inside a coloring tablet write a verse that applies to this week's lesson along the top of the first page. Example: "But the Lord is faithful. He will give you strength and protect you from the Evil One." 2 Thessalonians 3:3 NLT. Have them draw a picture of God protecting them from the Evil One. Add verses weekly and have them draw a picture to go along with the verse. This can be a coloring journal of scripture that you can read to them before bed.

- **For older children:** Using a set of spiral index cards or a journal, place scripture references applying to this week's devotional at the top of the first few pages. Help them look up the verses and write them on the card or page. Encourage them to read their Bible each day and write a verse in their index cards or journal. Talk with them about each verse. Remind them that God is a God of Truth and that His Word is truth. So, when the enemy tempts them to lie or believe a lie, all they have to do is get out their verses and read them.

Prayer: *Dear God, help me to know Your Word because it is true. Protect my heart and MIND against the lies of the Enemy. Please help me to be honest and never tell a lie because lies will hurt me and others. Amen!*

DAY 5

PREP FOR MOM...

We have talked about our brain/MIND, where it is, what is does, and the thoughts that begin in the MIND—good thoughts, bad thoughts, true thoughts, false thoughts, critical thoughts, mean thoughts, and hurtful thoughts. Today we will be talking about knowing God's Word. When we do scripture works like a protective gate around our thoughts.

Familiarize yourself with the following verses:

"How can a young person live a pure life? He can do it by obeying your word. With all my heart I try to obey you, God. Don't let me break your commands. I have taken your words to heart so I would not sin against you. Lord, you should be praised. Teach me your demands. I enjoy obeying your demands. And I will not forget your word." Psalm 119:9-12, 16 ICB

"My sheep hear My voice, and I know them, and they follow Me; and I give eternal life to them, and they will never perish; and no one will snatch them out of My hand." John 10:27-28 NASB

ACTIVITY PROPS AND SUPPLIES:

- White sheets of paper.
- Crayons or coloring markers
- Cotton balls
- Glue

SCRIPT FOR MOM...

Today we will be talking about knowing God's Word. When we do, His Word works like a protective gate around our thoughts.

Our verse today is: "How can a young person live a pure life? He can do it by obeying your (God's) Word. With all my heart I try to obey you, God. Don't let me break your commands.

I have taken your words to heart so I would not sin against you. Lord, you should be praised. Teach me your demands. I enjoy obeying your demands. And I will not forget your Word." Psalm 119:9-12, 16 ICB

This verse tells us that we are to know and obey God's Word—the Bible. When we know His Word our MINDS and hearts will be protected.

> **Question #1:** What are some things that protect us as a family? Possible answers: Daddy, fences, alarm system, policeman, etc.

If you have a fence around your yard, explain that the fence keeps out things that are unwanted, like other neighbor's dogs and many types of animals. If you have an alarm system, you might explain that it protects you and your family.

> **Question #2:** How does it make you feel knowing that because of daddy, our fences, the alarm system and policeman we have protection?

Did you know that when we have God's Word in our hearts and MINDS, it protects us, just as our fence and alarm system do?

Read: "My sheep hear My voice, and I know them, and they follow Me; and I give eternal life to them, and they will never perish; and no one will snatch them out of My hand." John 10:27-28 NASB

> **Question #3:** Do you know what a shepherd does? He takes care of the sheep— feeds them, watches over them and protects them.

Using the verse from John 10 explain that sheep know the voice of their shepherd. Sheep will not follow the voice of any other shepherd but their own. The job of the shepherd is to protect and care for the sheep. We are God's sheep and He is our shepherd. One of His names is The Great Shepherd. We want to be able to hear Jesus our Shepherd's voice. He speaks to us through His Word. We can know what Jesus says because the Bible is full of His thoughts!

We want to know His Word so our MINDS will be protected against false, bad, mean, critical and hurtful thoughts. The best way for us to think about what is true and pure is to have His Word in our MINDS.

> *When we know God's Word our minds and hearts will be protected.*

ACTIVITY:

- **For older children ages 6 and above:** Talk with your children about the importance of memorizing Scripture and how you, as a family, can accomplish this. You could write verses on index cards and place them in prominent locations around the house—on bathroom mirrors and the kitchen refrigerator. You could divide the family into teams of two and have a contest to see which team can memorize the verse first. Be creative and committed to developing the discipline of memorizing scripture as a family. Keep them easy and applicable to the ages of your children.

- **For younger children:** Use songs on CD or DVDs to teach them scripture. Young minds are very impressionable. They will never forget the scriptures they learn at a young age. The scriptures will "guard" and "protect" their MINDS—their thoughts. Note: Children's Scripture Resources: Steve Green's *Hide 'Em In Your Heart*, Seeds Family Worship Scripture CDs, and Rebecca Lutzer's *Awesome Bible Verses Every Kid Should Know*.

- Let the **younger children** color a picture of a shepherd and sheep. Glue the cotton balls on the sheep. Place the verse from John 10 in a simple version at the top and help them memorize it. (For example: "My sheep hear My voice, I know them, and they follow Me.") Give them a special treat for memorizing God's Word.

Prayer: *Dear God, thank you for being my Shepherd and my protector. Help me to know Your Word because it will help guard my mind against false, bad, mean, critical and hurtful thoughts. Amen!*

BUILDING A

Friendship

In this week's *Mommy and Me*, we will be talking about FRIENDSHIP. Our FRIENDSHIPS are some of the most important relationships we have because of how easily and fully they influence us. FRIENDSHIPS make life a little easier and a lot more fun.

God has not created us to live life all alone. He means for us to enjoy the sweet gift of companionship that offers help and encouragement. Our FRIENDSHIPS should be a reflection of Christ—they should help us to know Him better and become more like Him.

Using a variety of verses, we want to help the children see what the Bible teaches about being and choosing a friend. To help us better understand and remember what we learn, we'd like for you and your children to spend time this week 'Building a FRIENDSHIP' of your very own. Lego blocks are the perfect prop for this activity so set aside a bucket full just for *Mommy and Me* time.

Ready! Set! Build a FRIENDSHIP!

DAY 1

PREP FOR MOM...

This week we will be talking about FRIENDSHIP. We will be using large Lego blocks to "Build a FRIENDSHIP" each day this week. Get those Legos ready! Today, we will look at how to **choose** a friend—what God would have us look for in **choosing** a friend.

Familiarize yourself with the following verses:

"Whoever spends time with wise people will become wise. But whoever makes friends with fools will suffer." Proverbs 13:20 ICB

> *"Whoever spends time with wise people will become wise. But whoever makes friends with fools will suffer."*
> *Proverbs 13:20 ICB*

"Don't make friends with someone who easily gets angry. Don't spend time with someone who has a bad temper." Proverbs 22:24 ICB

"Iron can sharpen iron. In the same way, people can help each other." Proverbs 27:17 ICB

ACTIVITY PROPS AND SUPPLIES:

- Large Lego blocks (Any type of blocks would work for this activity)
- Dry-erase marker to write on Lego blocks
- One sheet of 8½ x 11 white paper
- #2 pencil

SCRIPT FOR MOM...

This week we are going to talk about FRIENDSHIP. In the Bible, the book of Proverbs was written by King Solomon and two of his friends. They wrote this book to give us practical suggestions for living—like how to **choose** a friend.

> **Question #1:** What is a friend? Let the child answer. (One attached to another by affection, fondness, love, esteem, or an acquaintance—someone we know well.)

Proverbs 13:20 says, "Whoever spends time with **wise** people will become wise. But whoever makes friends with fools will suffer." ICB

Question #2: Do you know what it means to be wise? Other words for wise: Insightful, smart, intelligent, brilliant, **thoughtful**, having deep understanding and sound judgment.

Did you know King Solomon was the wisest man in the world? Maybe we should listen to what he says on choosing friends—that being friends with wise people will make us wise, too.

Question #3: How can being friends with wise people make us wise?

Being friends with people who **want to know God better** will help us know God better, too. We share our toys, secrets, and our hearts and lives with our friends. Such things should only be trusted to people who will be a good friend and help us become more like Christ.

Solomon goes on to say, "Don't make friends with someone who easily gets angry. Don't spend time with someone who has a bad temper." Proverbs 22:24 ICB

Question #4: How do you know when someone has a bad temper? Why does Solomon say not to be friends with a person who gets angry easily or has a bad temper?

The Bible says that having a bad temper (being out of control) and anger are sin. A person who is angry, mean, and has a bad temper cannot be a good friend to anyone else. God wants us to choose friends who **act as God would have us act—calmly, lovingly and kindly.**

When choosing friends, we need to listen to Solomon's wise words when he says, "Iron can sharpen iron. In the same way, people can help each other." (Proverbs 27:17 ICB) In other words two friends who **work together** can help (or sharpen) each other to become better people.

Proverbs 27:9 says, "…good advice from a friend is sweet." (ICB) Choose friends who always help. Mommy and daddy want you to always do the right thing and to choose friends who will help.

ACTIVITY:

- Let's 'Build a FRIENDSHIP' to help us remember today's FRIENDSHIP words that are found in **bold** in the lesson. Using a dry-erase marker write the FRIENDSHIP words on the Lego blocks: **choose a wise friend, thoughtful, want to know God better, act as God would have us act**, and who **work together**.

- Explain that we have learned a lot today about what the Bible teaches about FRIENDSHIP! We learned that we need to **choose wise friends** who **want to know God better**—friends who help us become better people. The more we think about and practice these things, the better friend we will be and the better friends we will have! (Build the blocks as you talk.)

- Using a pencil, write the word FRIEND on white paper. Press hard to darken each letter. Put the pencil down and rub your hand across the word. What happens? The pencil lead rubs off onto you? This is what happens with our friends! They rub off on us, and we rub off on them. Being friends with someone means we will change each other. Now, why is it important to choose wise godly friends?

Prayer: *Dear God, friends are special and important. They make life more fun. Please help me choose friends that are wise and help me love You better! Amen!*

DAY 2

PREP FOR MOM...

Today we will be talking about **being** a friend. Familiarize yourself with the following verses:

Read through the story of David and Jonathan's FRIENDSHIP in preparation for today's devotional in 1 Samuel 18:1-4 and 20:11-42. Be prepared to summarize the story for your child.

ACTIVITY PROPS AND SUPPLIES:

- Large Lego blocks
- Dry-erase marker to write on Lego blocks

SCRIPT FOR MOM...

Today we will be talking about **being** a friend. Just what is a friend?

> **Question #1:** Where do we find friends?
>
> **Question #2:** Are friends important? Why?

Explain that FRIENDSHIPS are important. The dictionary defines *friend* as a person who you like and enjoy being with, a person who helps or supports someone or something. Doesn't that sound happy!

Talk with your child about their friends and your friends. Ask your child what he likes about a specific friend. Take turns telling things you like about those friends and sharing favorite stories about them.

Read the following verse:

"Some friends may ruin you. But a real friend will be more loyal than a brother." Proverbs 18:24 ICB

Question #3: What is a *real* friend? Be prepared to help your child define a *real* friend. Discuss the difference between *real* and *fake*. Re-read Proverbs 18:24 and emphasize the meaning of *real*.

The Bible is the best place to go to learn what it means to be a friend! It is full of examples of people who were good friends and people who were bad friends. In these stories, we see what to do and what not to do to be a good friend.

The story of Jonathan and David is a great example of friendship!

Summarize the story:

- David, the palace musician, and Jonathan, the royal prince, have become very best friends.
- Unfortunately, King Saul (Jonathan's father) is angry and wants to kill David.
- Jonathan **protects** David and helps him escape. He is a *real* friend to David.
- Jonathan and David did exactly what friends are to do—they **took care of** each other.

Question #4: What are some things you enjoy doing with your friends? Tell me about a time when you and your friend helped or **took care of** each other.

FRIENDSHIPS are very **special**, but to have a friend, we need to be a friend. When we are a friend to someone, they will in turn be a friend to us—as Jonathan and David were to each other.

The Bible says, "Do to others as you would like them to do to you." Luke 6:31 NLT

Question #5: Do you know what this verse is saying? Explain that the Bible says we should treat others—our friends—the same way we want to be treated. To **love** someone else as well as we **love** ourselves means we will treat that person very **special**! How do you **treat others special**?

Question #6: What **nice** things would you want a friend to do for you? What mean things would you not want a friend to do to you? Discuss what it means to be **kind**.

ACTIVITY:

- Let's 'Build a FRIENDSHIP' to help us remember today's FRIENDSHIP words that are found in **bold** in the lesson. Using a dry-erase marker write the FRIENDSHIP words on the Lego blocks: **protect, take care of**, be **kind, love,** be **nice** and **treat each other special.**

- As the child stacks the blocks, explain that we have learned a lot today about what the Bible teaches about FRIENDSHIPS! We have learned that friends **protect** and **take care of** each other. Friends are **kind** and **treat each other special.**

- The more we think about and practice these things, the better friends we will be and the better friends we will have!

Prayer: *Dear God, I am learning that friends are special and important. They make life more fun, and they help me know You better! Help me be the kind of friend the Bible says I should be. Amen!*

DAY 3

PREP FOR MOM...

Today, we are going to learn how to be a **loving** and **loyal** friend! Familiarize yourself with the following verses:

"This is my commandment: Love each other in the same way I have loved you. There is no greater love than to lay down one's life for one's friends. You are my friends if you do what I command…This is my command: Love each other." John 15:12-14 and 17 NLT

"A friend is always loyal, and a brother is born to help in time of need." Proverbs 17:17 NLT

"And Jonathan made a solemn pact with David, because he loved him as he loved himself." 1 Samuel 18:3 NLT

> *Jesus told His disciples to love each other the way He loved them. Jesus was a loving and loyal friend to His disciples. "A friend is always loyal, and a brother is born to help in time of need."* Proverbs 17:17 NLT

ACTIVITY PROPS AND SUPPLIES:

- Large Lego blocks
- Dry-erase marker to write on Lego blocks

SCRIPT FOR MOM...

Yesterday, we learned what it means to be a friend and we built our very own FRIENDSHIP using the Lego blocks. Today, we are going to learn how to be a **loving** and **loyal** friend!

Question #1: Do you remember what the Bible says about being a good friend—a *real* friend? Friends **protect** and are **kind**. They **take care of each other** and **treat each other special**.

The Bible talks about love from cover to cover. It's the most important theme in the Bible, so that means it should be the most important theme in our FRIENDSHIPS, too!

Read: "This is my commandment: Love each other in the same way I have loved you. There is no greater love than to lay down one's life for one's friends. You are my friends if you do what I command…This is my command love each other." John 15:12-14 and 17 NLT

Jesus tells His disciples to love each other the way He loves them. Jesus was a loving and loyal friend to His disciples.

Read: "A friend is always loyal, and a brother is born to help in time of need."
Proverbs 17:17 NLT

Question #2: What do you think the word *loyal* means? Faithful, dedicated, devoted, good.

- We know Jesus **loved** his disciples and was a **loyal** friend because he talked to them about God's love and helped them make good choices.

- He **served** them, made them meals, washed their feet, and healed their hurts. Sometimes the disciples were even unkind to Him. But, Jesus **loved** them so much He always **forgave** them.

- Because Jesus never changes, He is that same kind of friend to us, too!

Question #3: What does **loving** others the same way Jesus **loves** us look like in our FRIENDSHIPS? Can it be talking to our friends about God's love, helping them, serving them, and forgiving them? Explain that this may seem a little hard to do, but if Jesus tells us to do it, then He is going to help us do it!

The Bible says that "Jonathan made a covenant with David because he **loved** him as himself." A covenant is a very special promise you make with someone you **love**. **For older children:** When Mommy and Daddy got married, we made a marriage covenant with each other. We promised to always **love** each other as husband and wife and always be together.

Jonathan and David made a best friends covenant, promising to always be best friends, to **love** each another and be **loyal** to each other. In a true FRIENDSHIP, there must be **love** and **loyalty**.

ACTIVITY:

- Let's continue 'Building a FRIENDSHIP' to help us remember today's FRIENDSHIP words: love, loyal, serve, forgave

- As the child stacks the blocks, explain that we have learned a lot today about what the Bible teaches about FRIENDSHIPS! We have learned that friends **love** each other, are **loyal** to each other, **serve** each other and **forgive** each other.

- Today, let's put what we have learned into action and show a friend how much we **love** him. Discuss ideas and get the children involved in showing **love** to one of their friends. Depending on the age of your child, you may have to prompt him or give him ideas.

- Siblings should be our first best friends! God was brilliant to set things up this way! Talk about how being friends as siblings helps us learn to be good friends to other people. Help him find a way to show his sibling **love** today. As a parent, be intentional in cultivating your children's relationships with each other. It might be challenging because of age and personality—but it's doable!

Prayer: *Dear God, I am learning that friends are special and important. They make life more fun, and help me know You better! Please help me to be a loving and loyal friend. Amen!*

DAY 4

PREP FOR MOM...

Today we will be talking about what makes a **faithful** and **trustworthy** friend. Familiarize yourself with the following verses:

> *Since words come from our heart, to our mind and out our mouths, we must be careful to keep a happy heart.*

Read through the story of Noah, a friend of God, who was saved along with his family from the flood in Genesis chapter 6 thru 9:1. Note: Even though the Bible does not specifically call Noah a friend of God, their relationship and his actions suggest it.

When it comes to being a **trustworthy** and **faithful** friend, we must consider the tongue and how hurtful it can be related to our FRIENDSHIPS. So, we will look at the verses below:

"So also the tongue is a small thing, but what enormous damage it can do. A great forest can be set on fire by one tiny spark." James 3:5 TLB

"Let everything you say be good and helpful, so that your words will be an encouragement to those who hear them." Ephesians 4:29 NLT

ACTIVITY PROPS AND SUPPLIES:

- Large Lego blocks
- Dry-erase marker to write on Lego blocks

SCRIPT FOR MOM...

Yesterday, we learned how to be a loving and loyal friend. The Bible tells us that friends take care of each other and protect each other. They are kind and treat each other special. Friends always choose each other. They tell each other about God's love and help each other. Friends serve and forgive each other.

Today we're going to learn how to be a **faithful** and **trustworthy** friend! The word *faithful* means keeping your promise—someone who keeps his word!

> **Question #1:** What does it mean to be trustworthy? It means a person that you can rely on to do or provide what is right—someone you can count on!
>
> **Question #2:** Do you know the story of Noah? What can you tell me about Noah? This is what the Bible tells us about Noah:
>
> • Noah and God were very good friends.
>
> • It was a sad time because everyone else on earth did not want to be God's friend.
>
> • Noah walked with God every day, getting to know Him better and learning to trust Him more.
>
> • Noah grew to understand God and wanted to be a part of whatever God was doing.
>
> • The people ignored God, but not Noah. They lived however they wanted to, but Noah lived the way God wanted him to.
>
> • The people were mean and not sorry for their sin; God decided to start the world over by sending a flood.

Noah was a **faithful** and **trustworthy** friend that God could count on. God decided to save him from the flood! Noah spoke about God to the people. His words were kind and honoring of God because he wanted them to know Him as he did.

To be a **faithful** and **trustworthy** friend, we must watch what we say. "So also the tongue is a small thing, but what enormous damage it can do." James 3:5a (TLB) Explain that the tongue may be small, but it can hurt in a big way. We need to remember this in our FRIENDSHIPS and try hard to **speak good words** about our friends!

Read: "Let everything you say be **good** and **helpful**, so that your words will be an encouragement to those who hear them." Ephesians 4:29b NLT

> **Question #3:** What are some "**good** and **helpful**" words you can say to your friends? Friends do not talk badly to or about each other. They do not keep secrets or make mean jokes about each other. Friends **use their words to affirm and encourage** each other.

Since words come from our heart, to our mind and out our mouths, we must be careful to keep a happy heart. We can follow Noah's example. Because he had a happy heart and was a faithful and trustworthy friend, he had a very special FRIENDSHIP with God. In the end, this special FRIENDSHIP saved the lives of Noah and his family.

ACTIVITY:

- Using the Lego blocks, Build a FRIENDSHIP' to help remember today's FRIENDSHIP words: **faithful, trustworthy, good, helpful, speaks good words, and uses words to encourage**. Stack the blocks and talk about each word.

- Let's play the *Trust Game*. Have your child stand in front of you with his back to you with eyes closed. Without giving any **words of encouragement**, ask them to fall back and *trust* that you will catch them. Play the game again but speak **encouraging** words before you ask them to fall. Tell them sincerely how much you love them and assure them that you will catch them. Ask: Was it easier or harder to trust me after hearing **encouraging** words? A trustworthy person speaks **kind** and **encouraging** words.

Prayer: *Dear God, I am learning that friends are special and important. Please help me be a faithful and trustworthy friend. Guard my mouth and help me to use my words to encourage my friends. Amen!*

DAY 5

PREP FOR MOM...

Today we will talk about being a **kind** and **encouraging** friend. Familiarize yourself with the following verses:

"So encourage each other and build each other up, just as you are already doing."
1 Thessalonians 5:11 NLT

"Two people are better off than one, for they can help each other succeed. If one person falls, the other can reach out and help. But someone who falls alone is in real trouble."
Ecclesiastes 4:9-10 NLT

ACTIVITY PROPS AND SUPPLIES:

- Large Lego blocks
- Dry-erase marker to write on Lego blocks
- Space enough to stand in a circle for the Kindness Game

SCRIPT FOR MOM...

Yesterday, we learned how to be a **faithful** and **trustworthy** friend! Today we're going to learn how to be a **kind** and **encouraging** friend!

> **Question #1:** Thinking back on the stories of Jonathan and David, Jesus and His disciples and Noah, how did they show kindness to one another and encourage one another?
>
> **Question #2:** What does it mean to be **kind** to another person? What are some ways you show kindness to others? To be **kind** is to treat others with good manners and gentle consideration.

The Bible tells us that we are to "**encourage** each other and build each other up, just as you are already doing." 1 Thessalonians 5:11 NLT

Question #3: Do you know what it means to **encourage** someone? It means to spur on, to cheer for, to give help to, fortify or strengthen. To be **encouraging** is to give support or help that grows confidence and hope.

Give an example when you as a family **encouraged** another member of your family. Example: Child playing a sport, dad running in a marathon, etc.

A **kind** and **encouraging** friend is **unselfish**. He lets you be yourself. He helps you become the very best person you can. Everyone needs a **kind** and **encouraging** friend!

Question #4: Can you remember the FRIENDSHIPS we have talked about this week?

Help your child list them. Ask: How did Jonathan and David show kindness and encouragement to each other? How was Jesus kind and encouraging to His disciples?

Question #5: Tell me about one of your friends who is **kind** and **encouraging** like these were to one another.

Question #6: When have you been a **kind** and **encouraging** friend to someone?

Having a **kind** and **encouraging** friend means we will have company and **help** all along the way. In the Bible it says, "Two people are better off than one, for they can help each other succeed. If one person falls, the other can reach out and help. But someone who falls alone is in real trouble." Ecclesiastes 4:9-10 NLT

Question #7: Have you ever fallen on the playground and needed help getting up? Did you have a friend who was willing to help you? Tell me about it.

God wants us to have **kind**, **encouraging** and **helpful** friends, but He especially wants us to be this type of friend.

ACTIVITY:

- Using the Lego blocks, Build a FRIENDSHIP to help remember today's friendship words: **kind, helpful, encouraging** and **unselfish**. Stack the blocks and talk about each word.

- For a little extra fun today, let's play the *Kindness Game*. Everyone get into a circle and take turns saying something kind about each other.

- There are two rules: 1.) You must say something **kind** to everyone. 2.) You cannot say the same thing someone else said.

- At the end of the game, let each person share how the **kind** things that were said about him made him feel.

- Discuss how it would have made him feel if someone had said unkind things about him. Being **kind** and **encouraging** gives life!

Prayer: *Dear God, please help me be a kind and encouraging friend. And, help me to choose friends who are kind and encouraging. Amen!*

A Heart of Gratitude

In this week's *Mommy and Me*, we will be talking about GRATITUDE. The word gratitude means the state of being grateful or thankful. One of the first words a child learns is "mine." Children are born with a selfish nature. We must teach them, not only to share, but to have a heart of GRATITUDE and thankfulness.

Just as LOVE, SELF-CONTROL and CONTENTMENT are issues of the heart—so is GRATITUDE. The following verse from Psalms will be our launching point this week in teaching the children what God says about having a heart of GRATITUDE.

"The Lord is my strength and shield. I trust in Him with all my heart. He helps me, and my heart is filled with joy. I burst out in songs of thanksgiving." Psalm 28:7 NLT

GRATITUDE is learned. Parents must cultivate a heart of GRATITUDE within their child.

Ready! Set! A Heart of GRATITUDE!

DAY 1

PREP FOR MOM...

GRATITUDE (Gratefulness) is a mindset, or better yet, a HEART attitude set that should be modeled and cultivated in the everyday moments of our children's lives. GRATITUDE is more than just teaching a child to say "Thank you" in response to receiving a gift or getting help when needed; it is about opening their *spirit eyes* to the involvement of God's goodness in their "little" worlds. Let's journey together this week as we cultivate and nurture GRATITUDE in the hearts of our children.

Familiarize yourself with the following verses:

> *Gratitude is more than just teaching a child to say "Thank you" in response to receiving a gift or getting help when needed; it is about opening their spirit eyes to the involvement of God's goodness in their "little" worlds.*

"I come to the altar, O Lord, singing a song of thanksgiving and telling of all your wonders." Psalm 26:6b-7 NLT

"Give praise to the LORD, PROCLAIM HIS NAME; make known among the nations what he has done. Sing to him, sing praise to him; tell of all his wonderful acts. Glory in his holy name; let the hearts of those who seek the LORD REJOICE." PSALM 105:1-3 NIV

Today we will be talking about the mouth and how it is the "gateway to a heart of GRATITUDE." Be prepared to explain what a gateway is: an opening to a gate. A gateway must be open to pass through. Our mouths are gateways for praise. We open them and express praise and GRATEFULNESS to God.

"A good man brings good things out of the good stored up in his heart, and an evil man brings evil things out of the evil stored up in his heart. For the mouth speaks what the heart is full of." Luke 6:45 NIV

ACTIVITY PROPS AND SUPPLIES:

- Find a song on video about GRATITUDE/thankfulness that the children can learn today. Go to Google or YouTube and search for Children's Christian songs on GRATITUDE or thankfulness. (One good source is: www.seedsfamilyworship.com/music/catalog Family Seeds of Character Vol. 6: Song: Give Thanks based on Psalm 105:1-3)

- Sheet of paper

- A black pen

SCRIPT FOR MOM…

Lesson today: How do we express GRATITUDE? With your mouth you express GRATITUDE.

> **Question #1:** Ask the children if they know what the word GRATITUDE (gratefulness) means?
>
> Explain: While their responses may be different based on their ages, you might get responses such as, "saying thank you" or "saying the magic words." Try to prompt their thoughts to how they express GRATITUDE (gratefulness).
>
> **Question #2:** Now that we know what it is, how are some ways we can express GRATITUDE?

Read one of the following translations based on the child's age and ability to understand:

"I come to the altar, O Lord, singing a song of thanksgiving and telling of all your wonders." Psalm 26:6b-7 NLT (Telling and singing are ways we use our mouth to express GRATITUDE.)

"I will speak with the voice of thanks, and tell of all Your great works." Psalm 26:7 NLV

Explain that the gateway to a heart of GRATITUDE is through the mouth. A gateway is an opening to a gate and it must be open to pass through. Our mouths are gateways for praise. We open them and express praise and GRATEFULNESS to God.

Read: "A good man brings good things out of the good stored up in his heart, and an evil man brings evil things out of the evil stored up in his heart. For the mouth speaks what the heart is full of." Luke 6:45 NIV

If our heart is full of GRATEFULNESS (thanksgiving), then our mouths will express our GRATITUDE to God and others.

ACTIVITY:

- Using a blank sheet of paper and a pen, write down all the things the children are grateful for, and once your list is complete, make up a song about each one expressing your GRATITUDE with your mouths.

- Instead of making up your own song about all the things the children are GRATEFUL for, you can find a song on YouTube about GRATITUDE/thankfulness that the children can learn today.

- Challenge the children to express GRATITUDE with their mouths for the next five days as you intentionally cultivate and nurture a heart of gratitude in them this week. Close in prayer.

Prayer: *Dear God, thank you for my family, my home, my toys and the food you give us to eat. I am grateful. Help me to use my mouth as a gateway of praise and thanksgiving. Amen!*

DAY 2

PREP FOR MOM...

Yesterday we talked about *How* to express our GRATITUDE—with our mouths. Today we will move on to the *Who* of GRATITUDE: God. Above everyone and everything, we are to express our gratitude to God. He loves a thankful heart!

> *"Give thanks to the Lord, for He is good; His love endures forever."*
> *Psalm 107:1 NIV*

Familiarize yourself with the following verses:

"Give thanks to the Lord, for He is good; His love endures forever." Psalm 107:1 NIV

"Give praise to the LORD, PROCLAIM HIS NAME; make known among the nations what he has done. Sing to him, sing praise to him; tell of all his wonderful acts. Glory in his holy name; let the hearts of those who seek the LORD REJOICE." PSALM 105:1-3 NIV

ACTIVITY PROPS AND SUPPLIES:

- Words and tune for the song: *Praise Him, Praise Him, All ye Little Children*
- Your family favorite CD or DVD to worship and praise the Lord with today.

SCRIPT FOR MOM...

Yesterday we talked about *HOW* we are to show gratitude.

> **Question #1:** Do you remember *HOW*: With our mouths. Today we are talking about *WHO*.
>
> **Question #2:** Who is deserving of our thankfulness? God and Jesus

Explain that just as mommies and daddies love to hear words of GRATITUDE and thanksgiving from their children, God loves to hear words of GRATITUDE from His children.

Read the following verses:

The Bible says, "Give thanks to the Lord, for He is good; His love endures forever."
Psalm 107:1 NIV

And, another verse says, "Give praise to the LORD, PROCLAIM HIS NAME; make known among the nations what he has done. Sing to him, sing praise to him; tell of all his wonderful acts. Glory in his holy name; let the hearts of those who seek the LORD REJOICE." PSALM 105:1-3 NIV

Question #3: What are some ways we can express our GRATITUDE to God?

Explain to the children that singing and praising is a way we can thank God (express GRATITUDE) for all He has done for us.

ACTIVITY:

- **For young children**, sing this song of praise and thanksgiving: (If you are not familiar with the tune, Google *Praise Him, Praise Him, All ye Little Children*)

> *Praise Him, praise Him, all ye little children,*
> *God is love, God is love; (Repeat phrase once)*
> *Love Him, love Him, all ye little children,*
> *God is love, God is love.(Repeat phrase once)*
> *Thank Him, thank Him, all ye little children,*
> *God is love, God is love; (Repeat phrase and End)*

- **For older children:** Take a few minutes to express through song your thankfulness to God using your favorite Christian CD or DVD. Allow the kids to dance, raise their hands and freely worship and give praise and thanks to the Lord. You might Google or YouTube Chris Tomlin's song *Forever* which is written from our verse today in Psalm 107:1.

Prayer: *Dear God, the Bible tells us to show our* GRATITUDE *through praising and worshipping You. I am grateful that I can use my mouth to tell You how much I love You and how thankful I am for all You do for me. Amen!*

DAY 3

PREP FOR MOM...

Today we will be talking about *WHAT* we can be grateful for in our everyday lives. What are we to be grateful for? EVERYTHING

Earlier we talked about *How* to express our GRATITUDE: With our mouths. And, yesterday we talked about the *Who* of GRATITUDE: God.

> *Count your blessings, name them one by one, Count your blessings see what God has done! Count your blessings, name them one by one, Count your many blessings see what God has done.*

Remind the children that above everyone and everything we are to express our GRATITUDE to God. He loves a thankful heart! He wants us to see and acknowledge all that we have to be grateful for, like our house, food to eat, a car to drive, friends, etc.

Familiarize yourself with the following verse: (Emphasis on these four words today: *give thanks for everything*.)

"…singing psalms and hymns and spiritual songs among yourselves, and making music to the Lord in your hearts. And *give thanks for everything* to God the Father in the name of our Lord Jesus Christ." Ephesians 5:19-20 NLT

ACTIVITY PROPS AND SUPPLIES:

- A copy of the chorus from the song: *Count Your Blessings*
- Sheets of white paper
- Pens

SCRIPT FOR MOM...

Question #1: *How* are we to express our GRATITUDE: With our mouths. Yesterday we talked about the *Who* of GRATITUDE.

Question #2: Who are we to give thanks to? God.

Remind the children that above everyone and everything we are to express our GRATITUDE to God. He loves a thankful heart! He wants us to see and acknowledge all that He has done for us.

Today we will be talking about *WHAT* we can be GRATEFUL for in our everyday lives.

Our verse today is: (Emphasis on these four words today: *give thanks for everything*.)

"…singing psalms and hymns and spiritual songs among yourselves, and making music to the Lord in your hearts. And *give thanks for everything* (emphasis on these four words today) to God the Father in the name of our Lord Jesus Christ." Ephesians 5:19-20 NLT

Question #3: What does this verse say we are to be thankful or GRATEFUL for? Everything

ACTIVITY:

Today you have two choices for an activity. If the children are not too restless, you might want to do both.

- Challenge the children to a competition. If your family is large enough, you could even divide into teams. Pass out pen and paper. Using a timer, see who can make the longest list of things he is thankful for. If you have preschoolers, mark a column on the paper for each child and have him state things out loud that he is GRATEFUL for as you jot them down. The child with the longest list at the end of the allotted time wins! Emphasize EVERYTHING that is available to them. Ready. Set. GO! When time is up, compare lists and rejoice together about all the wonders and blessings given to your family by your Heavenly Father.

- If time allows, teach your children the chorus from a cherished old hymn, *Count Your Blessings*. The words are:

    Count your blessings, name them one by one,

    Count your blessings see what God has done!

    Count your blessings, name them one by one,

    Count your many blessings see what God has done.

Every time you sing the chorus, change the number working up to five. Have the children name that number of things they are grateful for.

Example: *Count your blessings, name them one by one.* Name one thing you are thankful for: **My bike**. Once you have sung the chorus through using the **number one** and naming **one thing**, change the next chorus to the **number two.** *Count your blessings, name them two by two.* Name two things you are thankful for: **My bike and scooter**. Repeat the words to the chorus until you have gone up to the number 5. Note: You can go to 10 if the children are enjoying the song.

Prayer: *Dear God, I have so much to be thankful for. If I listed everything there would not be a sheet of paper big enough. Thank you for being a big God who gives big gifts. Amen!*

DAY 4

PREP FOR MOM…

We have talked about *How* to express our GRATITUDE—with our mouths. We also discussed *Who* should receive our GRATITUDE—God. Yesterday, you talked with the children about *WHAT* we can be grateful for in our everyday lives: EVERYTHING

Today's topic is the *WHEN* of prayer. *WHEN* do we pray?

> *"Always be joyful. Never stop praying. Be thankful in all circumstances, for this is God's will for you who belong to Christ Jesus." 1 Thessalonians 5:16-18 NLT*

Familiarize yourself with the following verses:

"Always be joyful. Never stop praying. Be thankful in all circumstances, for this is God's will for you who belong to Christ Jesus." 1 Thessalonians 5:16-18 NLT

"You have turned my mourning into joyful dancing. You have taken away my clothes of mourning and clothed me with joy, that I might sing praises to you and not be silent. O LORD MY GOD, I WILL GIVE YOU THANKS FOREVER!" PSALM 30:11-12 NLT

We will be talking today about *WHEN* is a good time to pray and also about being GRATEFUL or thankful in ALL circumstances.

When God says ALL—He means ALL. Yet, at times there are situations in which it is hard to be GRATEFUL/thankful. Note: Direct the discussion toward the age of your children—the "little" world they live in.

ACTIVITY PROPS AND SUPPLIES:

- Drawing paper
- Crayons or colored markers

SCRIPT FOR MOM...

Begin your time today modeling gratefulness to God by leading your children in a prayer of thanksgiving. Thank Him for who He is and what He has done for your family.

Read the first verse for today:

"Always be joyful. Never stop praying. Be thankful in all circumstances, for this is God's will for you who belong to Christ Jesus." 1 Thessalonians 5:16-18 NLT

> **Question #1:** *WHEN* is a good time to give thanks? Always! We can pray at anytime and in any place or situation.

The verse tells us to always be joyful and never stop praying. We can pray all the time because God loves to hear our voices, just as mommy and daddy love to hear your voice.

> **Question #2:** Can you pray while you are playing at the park or running across the yard? Yes, you can. God is always listening.

The rest of the verse says, "Be thankful in ALL circumstances."

> **Question #3:** God says ALL, but do you think He means ALL? Yes, He does.
>
> **Question #4:** What are some situations (circumstances) or times when it is hard to give thanks? Give the children time to ponder. You may have to prompt the conversation with something like this: When your friend will not share his toy or when a friend knocks you down on the playground.

Read the second verse:

"You have turned my mourning into joyful dancing. You have taken away my clothes of mourning and clothed me with joy, that I might sing praises to you and not be silent. O LORD MY GOD, I WILL GIVE YOU THANKS FOREVER!" PSALM 30:11-12 NLT

- Explain that David was speaking of his sadness and how God turned it into "joyful dancing."
- When hard things happen (like when friends push you down on the playground), we are still to give God praise and thanks.

- If you know of someone who is going through a hard time, yet they are joyful because they are trusting God, share their story with your child.

ACTIVITY:

- Have each child draw a picture of a time when they found it hard to be grateful.(Such as one of the situations above.)

- Write Psalm 30:12, "O Lord my God, I will give you thanks forever!" across the top of his picture. Hang the picture in a prominent place and review the verse in the coming days.

- Remember our verse that said, "Be thankful in all circumstances, *for this is God's will for you* who belong to Christ Jesus." 1 Thessalonians 5:16-18 NLT

- Explain that God desires for us to thank Him not only for the good things in our lives but for the hard and sometimes bad things.

Prayer: *Dear God, when my feelings are hurt, I will praise and thank You for being with me. When hard things happen to me, I will look to You and be joyful, like David. Thank you for loving me. Amen!*

DAY 5

PREP FOR MOM...

Review the week's lessons:

- *HOW* to express our GRATITUDE: With our MOUTHS

- *WHO* we are to show our GRATITUDE: To GOD

- *WHAT* we can be grateful for in our everyday lives: EVERYTHING

- The *WHEN* of prayer. *WHEN* do we pray? In ALL circumstances.

Today we will be talking about *WHERE* to give thanks. Explain that church is not the only place *WHERE* we can show GRATITUDE and thanksgiving.

Familiarize yourself with the following verses:

"The Lord is my strength and shield. I trust in Him with all my heart. He helps me, and my heart is filled with joy. I burst out in songs of thanksgiving." Psalm 28:7 NLT

"Joy and gladness will be found there. Songs of thanksgiving will fill the air." Isaiah 51:3b NLT

"Shout with joy to the Lord, all the earth! Worship the Lord with gladness. Come before him, singing with joy. Acknowledge that the Lord is God! He made us, and we are his. We are his people, the sheep of his pasture. Enter his gates with thanksgiving; go into his courts with praise. Give thanks to him and praise his name. For the Lord is good. His unfailing love continues forever, and his faithfulness continues to each generation." Psalm 100 NLT

> *One of the most meaningful activities a family can do is to commit to a season of thankfulness together.*

ACTIVITY PROPS AND SUPPLIES:

- Five index cards, each with a different word written in bold black marker: *HOW, WHO, WHAT, WHEN and WHERE.*

- A solid colored helium balloon for each child (Balloons are a $1.00 at the Dollar Store®)

- Black fine tip marker

Script for Mom...

Using the 5 index cards, hold up one at a time and read the word. (If children are old enough, ask them to read the word). As each word is held up, see if the children can remember what they learned about each one. Lastly hold up the word *WHERE*.

Explain that today you will be talking about *WHERE* to give thanks. Note that church is not the only place *WHERE* we can show GRATITUDE and thanksgiving.

Read the following verses:

"The Lord is my strength and shield. I trust in Him with all my heart. He helps me, and my heart is filled with joy. I burst out in songs of thanksgiving." Psalm 28:7 NLT

"Joy and gladness will be found there. Songs of thanksgiving will fill the air." Isaiah 51:3b NLT

> **Question #1:** If church is not the only place where we can show GRATITUDE/thanksgiving, where are some places we can show GRATITUDE/thanksgiving? Example: In our home, while we are hiking in the woods or playing at the park, while we are swimming in the lake, etc.

There is a beautiful Psalm written by King David. In this Psalm he wants everyone to worship God and acknowledge His goodness—to praise (worship) and thank Him for all we have: good health, daddy's job, our home, each other, friends, teachers, etc. Read Psalm 100.

Activity:

• Our verse tells us to "fill the air with songs of thanksgiving." Air is all around us, so no matter where we are, at church, home, school, the park, the lake or hiking in the woods, we can show GRATITUDE to God.

• Give each child a helium balloon. Make sure they are all different colors in order to tell them apart. Have the child tell you a few things he is GRATEFUL for and write them carefully on the balloon with a black fine tip marker. Once their thanksgivings are written on the balloons allow them to release them into the air. Before long you will see that you have filled the air with your thanksgiving. Let the children watch the balloons drift away in the wind. (Older children can write on their own balloon.)

- For fun, end your time with singing the song below to the tune of *If You're Happy and You Know It.*

  If you're grateful and you know it say thank you.

  If you're grateful and you know it say thank you.

  If you're grateful and you know it let your heart and mouth show it.

  If you're grateful and you know it say thank you.

Prayer: *Dear God, I want my praise and thanksgiving to fill the air. No matter where I am, at church, home, school or at the park, I will thank You and praise You. Amen!*

EXPRESSING OUR

Love

In this week's *Mommy and Me,* we will be talking about LOVE. God's LOVE for us, our LOVE for Him, our LOVE for our family, neighbors and friends and our LOVE for those around the world.

At times, it can be hard to LOVE those around us as Jesus desires for us to do. This week we want the children to understand that LOVE comes from the heart. We can only truly LOVE others if Jesus lives in our hearts.

The following verse from Luke 10:27, will be our launching point this week in teaching the children what God has to say about LOVE.

Luke 10:27 says, "'You must love the Lord your God with all your heart, all your soul, all your strength, and all your mind.' And, 'Love your neighbor as yourself.'" Luke 10:27 NLT

> *"Love the Lord your God with all your heart, soul and mind. This is the first and most important command. And the second command is like the first: Love your neighbor as you love yourself."' Matthew 22:37-39*

Remember, Mom, you set the example for your children of how to LOVE as Christ desires for us to LOVE.

Ready! Set! Express LOVE!

DAY 1

PREP FOR MOM…

Today we will be talking about LOVING Jesus with our whole heart.

Familiarize yourself with the following verses:

"And you must LOVE the LORD your God with all your heart, all your soul, and all your strength." Deuteronomy 6:5 NLT

"The man answered, 'You must LOVE the Lord your God with all your heart, all your soul, all your strength, and all your mind.' And, 'LOVE your neighbor as yourself.'" Luke 10:27 NLT

Use Google sources or a library book on the human anatomy to find a picture of the human heart. Make sure the whole heart is visible (that the chambers and arteries are clearly shown). Print a copy for each child.

ACTIVITY PROPS AND SUPPLIES:

- Four sheets of construction paper- red and pink
- Heart-imprinted scrapbooking paper
- A black marker
- Tape or glue

SCRIPT FOR MOM…

Lesson today: LOVING Jesus with ALL your Heart

The Bible tells us that you are to LOVE God with all your heart.

Read Deuteronomy 6:5, "And you must LOVE the LORD your God with all your heart, all your soul, and all your strength." NLT

Using the sources found on Google and/or the book on the human anatomy, show the different parts of the heart. Explain that we cannot divide the heart into separate parts. We cannot remove a portion of the heart. If you remove a portion of the heart, a person cannot live.

We need ALL of our heart to live. We cannot live with half a heart, just as we cannot LOVE God with half our heart.

Question #1: Do you LOVE mommy and daddy with half your heart? Do you LOVE your brother/sister with half your heart? No, of course you don't. You LOVE them with your whole heart.

Question #2: What does it mean to LOVE God with ALL our hearts? Discuss.

In the book of Luke it says, "'You must LOVE the LORD your God with all your heart, all your soul, all your strength, and all your mind.' And, 'LOVE your neighbor as yourself.'" Luke 10:27, NLT

This means we are to LOVE God will **all** of our being—not half way—but with ALL of your heart! And, we are to LOVE others in the same way we LOVE God.

ACTIVITY:

- Help the children cut out pink and red construction paper hearts, all sizes. Note: A heart-shaped cookie cutter makes a great pattern.
- Write Luke 10:27 and the above Question #2 across an 8½ x 11 sheet of heart-imprinted scrapbooking paper. Write the children's answers below the question.
- Tape or glue the cut out hearts around the 8½ x 11 sheet making a border. Place the sheet on the refrigerator or in a prominent place.
- Discuss the reasons God asks us to LOVE Him with you whole heart.
- If you LOVE Him with your whole heart, you can LOVE others with your whole heart. Close in prayer.

Prayer: *Dear God, we do love You with our whole hearts and today we tell You that You are special to us. Amen!*

DAY 2

PREP FOR MOM...

Today we will be talking about how much God LOVES you and me

The Bible tells us that God LOVES us. But often we have a hard time believing that He LOVES us. We want the children to understand that God showed His love for them and the world by sending His Son, Jesus.

Familiarize yourself with the following verses:

"Even before he made the world, God LOVED us." Ephesians 1:4a NLT

"For this is how God LOVED the world: He gave his one and only Son, so that everyone who believes in him will not perish but have eternal life." John 3:16 NLT

"The Lord LOVES the godly." Psalm 146:8b NLT

ACTIVITY PROPS AND SUPPLIES:

- 5x7 framing mat with 4x6 opening—any color (Can be found in the framing section of any craft store.) Note: You may want to take the children to choose their own mats.
- 1 or 2 Packages of heart stickers
- 4 x 6 Picture of each child
- 12 inches colored ribbon
- Glue or tape
- 8-½ x 11 sheet of plain white paper
- Black marker

SCRIPT FOR MOM...

The Bible tells us that God LOVES us. Psalm 146:8a says, "The Lord LOVES the godly." NLT

In Ephesians it says, "Even before he made the world, God LOVED us." NLT

You and mommy and daddy were in the heart of God before He created the world.

Before you were born, mommy and daddy LOVED you. We had not seen you—but we LOVED you.

We know how much God LOVED us because He sent His very own Son, Jesus. The Bible says in John 3:16, "For this is how God LOVED the world: He gave his one and only Son, so that everyone who believes in him will not perish but have eternal life." NLT

> *We know how much God loved us because He sent His very own Son, Jesus.*

Sing the song: Jesus LOVES Me.

Question #1: What are some ways that God shows His LOVE for us? Discuss.

God sent His one and only Son, Jesus, to earth because He LOVES us. He LOVES you, your sister/brother, daddy, mommy and everyone in the world.

SCRIPTURE MEMORY:

- Cut an 8-½ x 11 solid white sheet of paper into strips. With a fine tip black marker write a phrase from the verse in John 3:16 on each strip until the entire verse has been written out.
- Give each family member a strip of paper.
- Each evening, use the strips containing the phrase from John 3:16 to help the family to memorize the verse. (Choose your version.)
- For more of a challenge: After the first night, remove one strip each evening until the family can say John 3:16 from memory. Note: If the family has already memorized John 3:16, consider using Ephesians 1:4, "Even before he made the world, God loved us and chose us in Christ to be holy and without fault in his eyes." NLT

ACTIVITY:

- Give each child a 5x7 mat with a 4x6 opening.
- Tape a 4x6 photo of each child onto the back of a mat. Picture should be showing through the front of the 4x6 opening.

- If there is room, write a verse from today's lesson across the top of the mat with a black marker.

- Let the children decorate the border of their mat with heart stickers.

- Tape or glue a ribbon from the back two top corners of the mat. Hang the mats in a prominent place in the house. Example: On the bedroom door of each child.

Tell each child how much you LOVE them and how much God LOVES them. They are special to you and to God. Close in prayer.

Prayer: *Dear God, thank you for loving me. I am special to You. Thank you for showing me how much You love me by sending your Son, Jesus. Amen!*

DAY 3

PREP FOR MOM...

Today we will be talking about how we are to LOVE one another.

Familiarize yourself with the following verses:

"LOVE each other as brothers and sisters." 1 Peter 3:8 NLT

"LOVE each other. Just as I have LOVED you, you should LOVE each other." John 13:34 NLT "This is My command: LOVE each other." John 15:17 NIV

"We should LOVE one another." 1 John 3:11 NIV

ACTIVITY PROPS AND SUPPLIES:

- One sheet of white poster board
- A black marker
- Kitchen chair

SCRIPT FOR MOM...

Question #1: What word have we been talking about in our lessons this week? LOVE

Question #2: Did you know that the Bible tells us to LOVE one another?

Read the verses below. Note: If your children are older, write the verses below on an index card prior to devotional time and allow each one to read a verse.

"LOVE each other as brothers and sisters." 1 Peter 3:8

"LOVE each other. Just as I (Explain that "I" is God speaking) have LOVED you, you should LOVE one another." John 13:34

"This is My command: LOVE each other." John 15:17 NIV

"We should LOVE one another." 1 John 3:11 NIV

God says that we are to LOVE one another. Mommy is to LOVE daddy, daddy is to LOVE mommy, we are to love you, you are to love us, and you are to love one another.

Question #3: Who sets an example for us in how to LOVE one another? God does. He says we are to LOVE one another as He has LOVED us.

We can only genuinely LOVE one another, if we LOVE God first. Our LOVE for God will help us to love one another.

Question #4: What are some ways we can show LOVE to one another? Discuss.

ACTIVITY:

- Consider doing this activity at dinnertime one evening. On a sheet of white poster board, write down each family members name in column form. Sample:

  Mommy   Daddy   Ella   Nicholas   Katie   Trip

- Ask each family member to think of things that they LOVE about one another. As you come to each name have the person you are speaking of stand on a kitchen table chair as the "honored" and "loved" family member.

- Write all the things said about each one under the appropriate name.

- Once you finish with one family member, have the next family member climb up on the chair until everyone has had a turn.

The Bible tells us to LOVE one another. We can only do this if we LOVE God first. Close in prayer.

Prayer: *Dear God, help us to love You with all our heart. Help us to love one another as You have loved us. Amen!*

PREP FOR MOM...

Today we will be talking about how and why we are to LOVE our "neighbor" as God loves us.

Familiarize yourself with the following verses:

> *"Love your neighbor as yourself."*
> *James 2:8b NLT*

"We LOVE each other because he LOVED us first." 1 John 4:19 NLT

"...but LOVE your neighbor as yourself. I am the LORD." Lev. 19:18 NLT

"LOVE your neighbor as yourself." James 2:8b NLT

Read through the story of the Good Samaritan in Luke 10:30-37 and be prepared to tell a summary version of the story to the children.

ACTIVITY PROPS AND SUPPLIES:

- A variety of paper, crayons, markers, etc. for making cards.
- Red pipe cleaners
- Heart-shaped beads (red, pink and white)
- Ingredients for baked good recipe of choice

SCRIPT FOR MOM...

Lesson today: God LOVES the world through us. Because He LOVED us, we are to LOVE—not just our family—but others.

Read the following verses aloud:

"We LOVE each other because he first LOVED us." 1 John 4:19 NLT

"...but LOVE your neighbor as yourself. I am the LORD." Lev. 19:18 NLT

Question #1: When God says to LOVE "your neighbor," who is He talking about? "Neighbor does not merely mean one who lives nearby, but anyone with whom one comes in contact." The NIV Study Bible

God says we are to LOVE the world—those living in the world—our neighbors, other children at school, our family and our friends. They will know we belong to Christ by the way we LOVE others.

Tell the story of the Good Samaritan in Luke 10:30-37:

- Discuss which character (The priest, Levite or the Samaritan) in the story LOVED the Jewish man.

- How did he show LOVE? Explain that the Jewish people and the Samaritan people did not like each other. But, because of this Samaritan's compassion, he could LOVE a man he was not even supposed to like.

Question #2: God helps us LOVE others. Who are the "others" around you that God wants you to LOVE? Example: School teacher, library personnel, firemen, policemen, neighbors, etc.

Question #3: If children are in school, ask how they can show LOVE to the other children in their class. Perhaps there is a child in their classroom that many of the children pick on or a child with special needs, ask how they can show LOVE towards that child.

Question #4: Ask how you as a family can LOVE and show Christ's LOVE to your neighbors. Example: If you have a widow in your neighborhood, bake cookies and deliver them to her. Close in prayer.

Prayer: *Dear God, thank you for LOVING us so that we can learn how to LOVE others. Give us eyes to see those at school, those in our neighborhood, and others we come in contact with while we are out running errands that need to be LOVED. Amen!*

ACTIVITY:

- Tell the children that you are going to show LOVE to your "neighbors" by making a craft (See idea below), coloring a picture, or preparing a baked good (recipe included in today's lesson) for a neighbor, school teacher, or the firemen at the local fire station.

- Attach a verse from today's lesson to your gift.

- Take the children to deliver the LOVE gift.

- Craft Idea: Using the heart shaped beads and pipe cleaners, thread several of the beads, using all three colors, onto the pipe cleaners. Children can make bracelets or book marks to give to those they desire to show LOVE.

DIANNE'S CHOCOLATE CHIP COOKIES

1 c butter-softened	1 t baking soda
¾ c light brown sugar	2 ½ c all-purpose flour
¾ c granulated sugar	1 c Ghirardelli milk chocolate chips
2 t vanilla	½ c Ghirardelli semi-sweet chocolate chips
2 eggs-room temperature	¾ c chopped pecans or walnuts-optional
1 t salt	1 bag Ghirardelli chocolate dipping wafers

Cream together butter, both sugars and vanilla until light and fluffy. Add eggs until blended. Add the salt, baking powder and flour. Mix until smooth. Fold in the chocolate chips and nuts. Bake at 325° for 8-10 minutes until golden brown. Remove to cooling rack. Once cool, melt chocolate dipping wafers according to instructions on bag. Dip half of the chocolate cookie into the coating and place on parchment paper to dry. Once the cookies are dry and the coating hardened, place in air-tight container. These make a beautiful and delicious gift for a "neighbor." Note: If you have small children, you may want to make the cookies ahead of time and then allow them to help with dipping the cookies.

DAY 5

PREP FOR MOM...

Today we will be talking about LOVING people around the world.

Familiarize yourself with the following verse:

We can only genuinely love one another, if we love God first.

"May the Lord make your LOVE for one another and for all people grow and overflow..." 1 Thessalonians 3:12 NLT

Using a globe or world map and a copy of *Operation World*, found at the local Christian Bookstore (or other mission book), talk with the children about how many people are in the entire world and how many of them have never heard about the LOVE of Jesus. Note: Another great resource is The Child's World Prayer Map found at http://www.ehc.org/free-prayer-maps.

Using Google research choose one of the following people (you may have your own "heroes of the faith" list) who left his/her home and loved ones to go to another part of the world to tell others about God's LOVE:

Corrie Ten Boom

Arthur and Wilda Mathews

William Carey

Gladys Aylward

ACTIVITY PROPS AND SUPPLIES:

- Book: *Operation World*
- Resource: *The Child's World Prayer Map*

SCRIPT FOR MOM...

Today we will be talking about LOVING People Around the World.

Before you get into today's devotional, review the things you have learned this week. See how many the children can recall:

- You are to LOVE Jesus with your whole heart.

- God LOVES you and me.

- We are to LOVE one another (as a family).

- We are to LOVE our neighbor as God LOVES us.

> *"It is Christmas every time you let God love others through you." Mother Teresa*

The Bible talks about us LOVING all people—those closest to us, those around our city and those around the world. It says, "May the Lord make your LOVE for one another and for all people grow and overflow..."
1 Thessalonians 3:12 NLT

- We are not only to LOVE people around the world, but we are to pray for them continually. That means all the time.

- "So we have not stopped praying for you since we first heard about you. We ask God to give you complete knowledge of his will and to give you spiritual wisdom and understanding. Then the way you live will always honor and please the Lord, and your lives will produce every kind of good fruit. All the while, you will grow as you learn to know God better and better." Colossians 1:9-10 NLT

- Tell the children about one of the missionaries you researched and how he obeyed God's Word and went around the world to tell others about God's LOVE.

Question #1: Why does God ask us to LOVE and pray for people in other countries?

- If you as a family support any missionaries, orphans, or others, tell the children why you give to these in need. Their needs are not only physical—needing food, clothing, education, etc., but they also have a spiritual need. They need to know about the LOVE of Christ.

- If the mission ministry you support has a web-site, take the children to the web-site to see pictures, a picture is worth a thousand words!

- If you, your husband or a family member has been on a mission trip, tell the children about the trip and how God worked through those who went to show His LOVE to others. Show pictures, if you have them.

ACTIVITY:

- Call your church or a local mission organization to obtain the name and address of a missionary family. Have your children draw pictures for them and write a letter telling them that you as a family will be praying for them. If possible, obtain a picture to place on your refrigerator or in a prominent place as a reminder to pray for them.

- Using *Operation World* or *The Child's World Prayer Map* (http://www.ehc.org/free-prayer-maps), choose a country to pray for in the coming week. One evening decorate the kitchen in décor from the country you have chosen, dress as they dress, and prepare a meal with the ethnic food eaten in that country

- At dinner pray for the country you have chosen. Pray for those who live there and do not know Christ. Pray God will send missionaries to tell the people about Jesus and how much He LOVES them. Close in prayer.

- For informing your children about those who have answered the call to go and tell the good news of Christ, see the book series titled *Christian Heroes: Then and Now* by YWAM at P.O. Box 55787 Seattle, WA. 98155

- Book to use with young children ages 8-12: *You Can Change the World* by Jill Johnstone

- See *DesiringGod.org* for articles on missions for children.

Prayer: *Dear God, thank you that we live in a country where we can go to church. Thank you that we can sing and read about You in the Bible. Help all the people around the world to hear about You, Your son, Jesus, and His love for them. Send people to tell them and send Bibles to them so they can read about You. Amen!*

Showing Honor and...

Respect

In this week's *Mommy and Me*, we will be talking about RESPECT and what it means.

In the late 1960's, a song was written for Aretha Franklin, an African American Rock & Roll singer. The title of the song was R.E.S.P.E.C.T. This song was a top hit for Aretha and remains a popular song to this day. The reason being—we all want to be RESPECTED!

The word RESPECT means having high or special regard for someone. Synonyms for RESPECT are appreciation, esteem, favor, fondness, and love.

Contrary to what some people might believe, RESPECT is earned and learned! Children learn by example. If you talk poorly about a relative, the pastor, or people in positions of authority, your children will echo what they hear—they will learn DISRESPECT from you.

But, if you show RESPECT to your parents (grandparents), your pastor, and those in positions of authority, your children will as well.

We must be honorable, kind, honest, and trustworthy if we want others to RESPECT us.

God's Word says that we are to: "Be devoted to one another in love. Honor (respect) one another above yourselves." Romans 12:10 NIV

Ready! Set! Show RESPECT!!

DAY 1

PREP FOR MOM...

Familiarize yourself with the following verses:

"Honor the LORD from your wealth and from the first of all your produce."
Proverbs 3:9 NASB

"…so that all will honor the Son even as they honor the Father. He who does not honor the Son does not honor the Father who sent Him." John 5:23 NASB

This week you will be introducing your child to a word that might be "foreign" to him: RESPECT. You will want to be familiar with the definition of RESPECT and know synonyms of RESPECT.

Respect begins in our hearts and it shows the importance we place on something or someone.

Today, we want to focus on ways in which we can show honor and RESPECT to God. In the Bible, the word honor and RESPECT are interchangeable. In the above verses, we could replace the word *honor* with the word RESPECT.

When we honor or RESPECT God, we are demonstrating the high regard we have for Him and His ways. By honoring and RESPECTING Him, we are reflecting His glory back as praise and worship.

ACTIVITY PROPS AND SUPPLIES:

- A sheet of 8 ½ x 11 white paper for each child
- Colored markers
- Older Children: Construction paper and glue sticks

SCRIPT FOR MOM...

Lesson today: Showing Honor and Respect to God

Explain that when we honor and RESPECT God, we are showing our love for Him and His ways. RESPECT begins in our hearts and it shows the importance we place on something or someone. The Bible says about our heart:

"Blessed are the pure in heart, for they will see God." Matthew 5:8 NIV

"Above all else, guard your heart for everything you do flows from it." Proverbs 4:23 NIV

When something, like water, is pure, it is clean. We are to have a clean heart. We are also to guard our hearts. That means we are to protect it from bad things: thoughts, actions, lying, etc.

Help your child think of ways to show honor and RESPECT to God. Things such as: praying to Him, reading His Word, obeying His Word, and making good choices.

In Revelation, we read some very powerful words that express great honor toward God. It says, "Worthy are You, our Lord and our God, to receive glory and honor and power; for You created all things, and because of Your will they existed, and were created." Revelation 4:11 NASB

Because God is the Creator of the whole earth and rules over the earth, we are to honor and RESPECT Him.

ACTIVITY:

- Taking an 8 ½ x 11 sheet of white paper (for each child), across the top write these words: *Ways to Show* RESPECT *to God,* and at the bottom write *"Worthy are You, our Lord and our God, to receive glory and honor."*

- With markers, make a variety of large colored circles randomly on the sheet. Note: If children are old enough cut circles out of colored construction paper, glue them on the paper

- Around the perimeter of each circle write words such as: Home, School, Playground with Friends, Sports/Games, Grandparent's home and Church.

- Ask the child ways he can show RESPECT to God while at these places.

- Write their responses in the appropriate circle.

- Post in a place where the child will be reminded of his answers.

Prayer: *Dear God, I want to honor You with my whole heart. Protect my heart from bad things. Help me to remember that when I honor and RESPECT You, You are pleased. Amen!*

Explain: In the Bible, we are told to RESPECT our fathers and mothers, the elderly (older people), and those who rule over us. This week mommy will be talking to you about all the people we are to show RESPECT. We are going to have a fun week!

PREP FOR MOM...

Familiarize yourself with the following verses:

> *Showing respect means you are practicing obedience to God's Word.*

"Honor your father and mother (which is the first commandment with a promise) so that it may go well with you and that you may enjoy long life on the earth."
Ephesians 6:2-3 NASB

"Be devoted to one another in love. Honor (respect) one another above yourselves."
Romans 12:10 NIV

Mom, check your own heart before starting today. Do you show honor and RESPECT to your parents, pastor, in-laws, neighbors, sales clerks, and people in places of authority, etc.?

If you have failed to be the example you desire to be, it is not too late. God is waiting to forgive you and help you start fresh. **For older children**: You, mom, might apologize for not being the example you desire to be and tell them, with God's help, you are starting fresh.

ACTIVITY PROPS AND SUPPLIES:

- One sheet white poster board
- Colored markers

SCRIPT FOR MOM...

Lesson Today: Respecting your Parents

Read the following verses:

"Children obey your parents in the Lord, for this is right. Honor your father and mother (which is the first commandment with a promise), so that it may go well with you, and that you may live long on the earth." Ephesians 6:1-3 NASB

"Be devoted to one another in love. *Honor* one another above yourselves." Romans 12:10 NIV

In the Bible, the word honor and RESPECT are interchangeable. This means that where the word **honor** appears we could put the word RESPECT in its place.

Let's re-read the verses above and place the word RESPECT where the word honor is used.

Question #1: What are some ways you can show RESPECT to mommy and daddy? What are some ways you show disrespect toward mommy and daddy?

Give your child an example of ways he can show *verbal* and *nonverbal* respect. Example: Picking up your toys or saying yes ma'am/no ma'am when asked to do something.

The words "*Honor* (RESPECT) your father and mother" and "Children *obey* your parents" are commandments from God. He also gives us a promise in this verse. A promise is an oath, pledge, vow, or giving your word. What is the promise?

God keeps His word and He says that if you will obey and show RESPECT to your mommy and daddy, things will go well with you.

Question #2: What happens when you disobey and are disrespectful to mommy and daddy?

Things do not go well, do they?

Remind your children that showing RESPECT means you are practicing obedience to God's Word. Tell them that it makes God happy when we RESPECT and obey our parents. "Children, always obey your parents, for this pleases the Lord." Colossians 3:20 NLT

ACTIVITY:

- At the top of a white piece of poster board write: RESPECT STARTS WITH ME.
- Draw several large red hearts randomly around the board.
- Explain that when we are respectful, it reveals a kind heart and when we are disrespectful, it reveals an unkind heart.

- Ask each child to share with you ways he can show RESPECT toward you and your husband. Write each answer inside each heart. If you want, write the child's name around the exterior of the heart.

- Along the bottom of the poster board write: Honor your father and mother with your whole HEART.

If time allows, and children are old enough, role play ways to show RESPECT toward parents. Close your time by leading your child in the following prayer.

Prayer: *Dear God, I know the Bible tells me to honor,* RESPECT, *and obey my parents. Help me to have a kind heart and show* RESPECT *to my parents and others around me. Amen!*

DAY 3

PREP FOR MOM...

Review the verse in Romans from Day 2: "Be devoted to one another in love. Honor (respect) one another above yourselves." Romans 12:10 NIV

Familiarize yourself with the following verse:

"Do your best to live in peace with everyone." Romans 12:18 ICB

Children love to hear stories about when their parents were growing up. If you grew up with a sibling, tell a story of a time that you were disrespectful toward a sibling or vice versa. Talk about the way your parents handled the situation and the lesson you and your sibling learned.

ACTIVITY PROPS AND SUPPLIES:

- 8 ½ x 11 blank white paper
- White poster board
- Black marker

SCRIPT FOR MOM...

Lesson today: Respecting Siblings and Friends

Read the following verse:

"Be devoted to one another in love. Honor one another above yourselves." Romans 12:10 NIV

Remind the child that the word honor also means RESPECT.

Review: In the Bible, the word honor and RESPECT are interchangeable. This means that where the word honor appears we could put the word RESPECT in its place. Let's re-read the verse above and place the word RESPECT where the word honor is used.

God says that as a family, and as brother and sister, (whatever siblings are in the family) are to be devoted (which means loving or loyal) to one another. We are also to be devoted (loving or loyal) to our friends. When we love someone, we show him RESPECT.

"Do your best to live in peace with everyone." Romans 12:18 ICB

This means: Do not fight with one another. When we show RESPECT for one another, we will have peace in our home. We will have less fighting!

Question #1: What are some specific ways you can show honor or RESPECT to one another as siblings?

Question #2: What are some ways that you have been disrespectful to one another?

Question #3: When you are disrespectful, what should you do? Apologize!

The Bible tells us to treat others the way we want to be treated. So, if we want our friends to be kind and respectful to us, we need to be kind and respectful to our friends. Right?

Question #4: When you are playing with your friends at school, at their houses or here at our home, how can you show RESPECT toward them?

What if you are invited to a friend's home for dinner or to play? What are some ways you could show respect and courtesy when you first arrive? While you are playing? At their dinner table? When you leave?

ACTIVITY:

There are 3 options today:

- **For older children:** Work alone or with a sibling to create a song, a rap, or a chant about RESPECT. Your words should tell why respect is important and how it could make your family relationships and friendships better. Write the song or rap on a piece of paper and be ready to perform it for the family at dinnertime.

- **For younger children:** Make a happy face and sad face on paper and give each to your child. Describe to them different situations that show RESPECT or disrespect. Have the

child hold up the sign for how it makes them feel—the happy face for an example of respect and a sad face for an example of disrespect.

- **For all ages:** Using a white poster board write the word RESPECT at the top then draw a line down the middle. Label one side: LOOKS LIKE and the opposite side: SOUNDS LIKE. Thinking about what RESPECT should look like and sound like, make a list on each side. Example: LOOKS LIKE: Waiting your turn. SOUNDS LIKE: Saying Please. Have fun making the list together then end with this prayer:

Prayer: *Dear God, thank you for my _____ (brother's/sister's name) and thank you for my friends,_____ . Help me to love them, be kind to them, and show them RESPECT. Amen!*

DAY 4

PREP FOR MOM...

Familiarize yourself with the following verses:

"In the same way, you who are younger must accept the authority of the elders. And all of you, dress yourselves in humility as you relate to one another, for God opposes the proud but gives grace to the humble." 1 Peter 5:5 NLT

"Stand up in the presence of the aged, show respect for the elderly and revere your God. I am the Lord." Leviticus 19:32 NIV

In preparation, you might think back to your childhood and times you had with your grandparents. Be prepared to share a story or two of an occasion where you showed RESPECT to your grandparents.

The emphasis today is not only on children showing RESPECT to their grandparents but to the elderly. Depending on the age of the child, you may have to define *elderly* prior to talking about how to show them RESPECT.

ACTIVITY PROPS AND SUPPLIES:

- Bright colored 8½ x 11 sheets of paper
- Glue
- Glitter
- Black marker

> "Stand up in the presence of the aged, show respect for the elderly and revere your God. I am the Lord." Leviticus 19:32 NIV

SCRIPT FOR MOM...

Lesson Today: Respecting Grandparents and the Elderly

Read the following verses:

"In the same way, you who are younger must accept the authority of the elders. And all of you, dress yourselves in humility as you relate to one another, for God opposes the proud but gives grace to the humble." 1 Peter 5:5 NLT

"Stand up in the presence of the aged, show respect for the elderly and revere your God. I am the Lord." Leviticus 19:32 NIV

Question #1: Do you know what the word *elder* or *elderly* means? Discuss.

Explain the above verses in simple terms. Example: God's Word is saying that as young people you are to show honor and respect toward the elderly. You are to be humble and loving toward them.

Question #2: Can you name a few elderly people that we know?

Question #3: What are some ways you can show respect toward them?

We are to show RESPECT to the elderly and to our grandparents.

If you have a story of a way in which you showed RESPECT to your grandparents when you were young, share it with your child.

Question #4: What are some ways you can honor and show RESPECT to your grandparents?

Examples: Write them a note (or color a picture if too little to write) when they do something nice for you, obey them, help them around their house when visiting, open the door for them (if big enough), call or text them to see how they are doing, say thank you when they do something for you, etc.

For younger children: Read a children's book about RESPECT, i.e., *Berenstein Bears Show Respect*. Discuss the book and apply the principles to respecting the elderly and grandparents.

ACTIVITY:

Note: For younger children, mom will need to write the words and the child can sprinkle the glitter.

- Write the following verse on the top of your 8½ x 11 papers: "Stand up in the presence of the aged, show respect for the elderly and revere your God. I am the Lord." Leviticus 19:32 NIV

- Use glue to write on bright-colored paper a few statements that respectful children say or do to put a smile on an elderly person's or grandparent's face.

- Carefully sprinkle the letters with glitter and let them dry. Remove all excess glitter.

- You've made a perfect gift for an elderly friend of the family or a grandparent.

- Close out your time by praying for the elderly/grandparents in your life.

Prayer: *Dear God, thank you for _____. I am so glad you gave us elderly friends and grandparents. Help me to show _____, kindness and* RESPECT *because it pleases You. Amen!*

DAY 5

PREP FOR MOM...

Familiarize yourself with the following verses:

"Let everyone be subject to the governing authorities, for there is no authority except that which God has established. The authorities that exist have been established by God." Romans 13:1 NIV

"Show respect to all men. Love the Christians. Honor God with love and fear. Respect the head leader of the country." 1 Peter 2:17 NLV

We are to respect people in authority, just as we are to respect God, who is the ultimate authority.

Today, you will be discussing RESPECT to those outside our family and in places of authority or service within your community.

ACTIVITY PROPS AND SUPPLIES:

- Blank white 8 ½ x 11 paper or white card stock cut into 4x8 inch strips (in order to make bumper stickers for their bikes, tricycle, etc.).

SCRIPT FOR MOM...

Lesson today: Showing RESPECT to those outside our family.

Read the verses: "Let everyone be subject to the governing authorities, for there is no authority except that which God has established. The authorities that exist have been established by God." Romans 13:1 NIV

"Show RESPECT to all men. Love the Christians. Honor God with love and fear. RESPECT the head leader of the country." 1 Peter 2:17 NLV

Explain these verses in terms that your child will understand. Be sure to discuss what "authorities" means. Definition: power to influence, person in charge.

The first thing children need to understand is that God is the ultimate (final or utmost) authority. He made us, and we are His. (Psalm 103:19) All other authorities are under His authority. He is the boss!

Talk about how he is to RESPECT people in authority, just as he is to RESPECT mommy and daddy who are his authority—just as we are all to RESPECT God, who is the ultimate authority.

Remind the child that we are also to show RESPECT to those in places of service, i.e., sales clerk, waitress, postal worker, trash collector, etc.

Question #1: Who are some people we come in contact with in places of authority and who serve us we should RESPECT?

Example: Teachers, principals, doctors, nurses, Sunday School teachers, pastor and staff, clerks at the store, community workers, i.e., policeman, fireman, the trash collector, postal worker, etc.

Remind the child of what these people do for them and the community you live in.

Question #2: What do you think would happen if we did not have these people.

Discuss what our community would be like if we did not have them. Reinforce the need for everyone to treat all these important people with RESPECT.

For fun: Print off coloring pictures from the internet of policeman, fireman, teachers, etc, or have your child draw a picture of one of these important people and how he can show RESPECT toward them. Note: To reinforce what you have talked about today, take the picture your child drew along with a baked treat to the closest police or fire station.

ACTIVITY:

- Using blank white 8 ½ x 11 paper or white card stock cut into 4x8 inch strips in order to make bumper stickers for their bikes, tricycle, etc.

- Allow the children to decorate these related to showing RESPECT to community workers and service people.
- Attach them to their bike or tricycle with tape.

Before you pray, review all the people we should show RESPECT who were talked about this week.

Prayer: *Dear God, thank you for being my boss. Help me to show others* RESPECT—*to treat them kindly, to love and appreciate them as You do. Amen!*

PRACTICING
Self-Control

In this week's *Mommy and Me,* we are going to talk about SELF-CONTROL. Webster's defines it as restraint exercised over one's impulses, emotions or desires. Restraint is defined as control over the expression of one's emotion or thoughts. Well, to sum it up, SELF-CONTROL is controlling or restraining self!

Mommies often go without sleep, carry a great deal of responsibility within the home, and bear the weight of nurturing and overseeing the children. Therefore, when we are tired, we may lack SELF-CONTROL. I believe there is nothing like having children to test your ability to control yourself. Little people do not mean to test you in the area of SELF-CONTROL—they just do!

> *"But the Holy Spirit produces this kind of fruit in our lives: love, joy, peace, patience, kindness, goodness, faithfulness, gentleness, and self-control. There is no law against these things!"*
> *Galatians 5:22-23 NLT*

If you have read or studied the verse in Galatians 5 speaking of the fruit of the spirit, you will see that SELF-CONTROL is listed. "But the fruit of the Spirit is love, joy, peace, patience, kindness, goodness, faithfulness, gentleness, and SELF-CONTROL. Against such things there is no law." Galatians 5:22-23 NIV

God lists eight fruit and then ends with a ninth one: SELF-CONTROL. Truly, if we would allow the Holy Spirit to bear out the first eight in our lives, the ninth one would come much more easily to us. There are many areas in life where we have to practice SELF- CONTROL. We, as mommies, tired or not, must set the example.

This week we are going to talk with the children about having SELF- CONTROL over our words, feelings, and actions.

Ready! Set! *Self-Control*!

DAY 1

PREP FOR MOM...

SELF-CONTROL is defined as *control over your feelings or actions*. We often cannot choose what circumstances come our way, but we CAN choose how we respond to them. I find this is where self-control plays the biggest part for children. Self-control does not come naturally; it is very much a habit we have to work towards daily, and honestly, sometimes minute to minute.

Familiarize yourself with the following verses:

"But the Holy Spirit produces this kind of fruit in our lives: love, joy, peace, patience, kindness, goodness, faithfulness, gentleness, and SELF-CONTROL. There is no law against these things!" Galatians 5:22-23 NLT

> *When we are not careful to have self-control it affects us and those around us.*

"A person who does not quickly get angry shows that he has understanding. But a person who quickly loses his temper shows his foolishness." Proverbs 14:29 ICB

ACTIVITY PROPS AND SUPPLIES:

- Cup or glass
- Liquid dishwashing detergent
- 2 tablespoons of baking soda
- Vinegar
- Red food coloring (optional)
- Baking pan (or do this in the sink)

SCRIPT FOR MOM...

Today we are going to talk about having SELF-CONTROL. Read: "But the Holy Spirit produces this kind of fruit in our lives: love, joy, peace, patience, kindness, goodness, faithfulness, gentleness, and SELF-CONTROL. There is no law against these things!" Galatians 5:22-23 NLT

In the Bible the word *fruit* is used for qualities or good things in our lives. Fruit is good for us, isn't it? Does an apple tree grow grapes? No! Does a pear tree grow lemons? No!

Explain: Just as an apple tree does not grow grapes but grows apples, and a pear tree does not grow lemons, but grows pears, we are to grow "good" fruit because Jesus lives in our hearts. The *fruit* or good things—love, joy, peace, patience, kindness, goodness, faithfulness, gentleness, and SELF-CONTROL—can only happen if we have Jesus living in our hearts.

> **Question #1:** What is the last fruit listed in the verse we read? SELF-CONTROL
>
> **Question #2:** When mommy tells you that you need to have SELF-CONTROL, what does that mean?

Explain: *Self-control* is having control over your feelings or actions. There are a lot of times in our lives when we have to control our feelings and what we say and what we do. When we are not careful to have SELF-CONTROL, it affects us and those around us.

> **Question #3:** Can you think of a time when you did not use SELF-CONTROL? Let's talk about a time when you said something or did something that was hurtful to you or someone else because of your lack of SELF-CONTROL.

Explain: We need SELF-CONTROL for our actions so we don't get hurt. When we do not have SELF-CONTROL our anger can flare up, and we can get ourselves into messes that sometimes can hurt others.

The Bible tells us that when we do not control our anger, we show great foolishness. It says, "A person who does not quickly get angry shows that he has understanding. But a person who quickly loses his temper shows his foolishness." Proverbs 14:29 ICB

> **Question #4:** What do you think would happen if we didn't ever use SELF-CONTROL in the things we said or did?

ACTIVITY: *When You're About to Explode!*

- We are going to do a simple experiment to show how our anger can grow and hurt others. Read to your child the verse in Proverbs that discusses anger.

- Fill the cup or glass almost full with warm water. Add several drops of the red food coloring and a few drops of the liquid detergent. Add 2 tablespoons of baking soda. Slowly pour vinegar into the glass and jump back quickly!

- A chemical reaction has just happened. When baking soda and vinegar mix, it produces a chemical reaction, which produces carbon dioxide—the same gas that bubbles in a real volcano. The gas bubbles build, causing the liquid to overflow. This reminds me of how a lack of SELF-CONTROL works in us!

- Ask your child: How does this remind you of anger? What are some things that can happen when you get angry? What can you do when you are about to lose self-control?

Prayer: *Jesus, I know that You understand what it is like to be a kid and how hard it is sometimes to have* SELF-CONTROL. *When I do not have* SELF-CONTROL, *remind me to stop, breathe, and pray so that I can control my words and actions. Amen!*

DAY 2

PREP FOR MOM...

Remember, SELF-CONTROL is defined as control over your feelings or actions. Today we are going to discuss how having self-control can be a protection to us and how lacking SELF-CONTROL can harm us.

Familiarize yourself with the following verses:

"A man without SELF-CONTROL is like a city broken into and left without walls."
Proverbs 25:28 ESV

> *We can ask God to help us with our self-control.*

"In the future I will make this agreement with the people of Israel, says the Lord. I will put my teachings in their minds. And I will write them on their hearts. I will be their God, and they will be my people."
Hebrews 8:10 ICB

ACTIVITY PROPS OR SUPPLIES:

- Pillows
- Sheets and blankets
- Chair(s)
- Any other item to build a fort

SCRIPT FOR MOM...

> **Question #1:** What fruit of the Spirit did we talk about yesterday? That is right! SELF- CONTROL.

The Bible says, "A man without SELF-CONTROL is like a city broken into and left without walls." Proverbs 25:28 ESV

Question #2: Have you ever played *King of the Castle* also known as *King of the Hill?* The object of the game is to stay on top of a large hill or any other designated area, as the "King of the Castle (Hill)." Other players attempt to knock the current King off the pile and take his place, thus becoming the new King of the Castle (Hill).

Question #3: Kings actually live in castles and not on hills. What is it that surrounds a castle to protect the King and all those within the castle? WALLS

Explain: In the Bible and long ago, people used to build walls around their cities to protect them from wicked and dangerous enemies. Think about the fences that we have in our yards. These fences protect our animals, our possessions, and keep people and other animals out.

Question #4: What would happen when the walls of a city were knocked down? The people would be attacked and hurt.

Question #5: Do you remember the story of Joshua and the battle of Jericho? What happened to the walls after Joshua and the people marched around the city seven times? The walls fell, didn't they?

Read: "Then the Lord spoke to Joshua. He said, "Look, 'I have given you Jericho, its king and all its fighting men. March around the city with your army one time every day. Do this for six days…On the seventh day march around the city seven times. On that day tell the priests to blow the trumpets as they march. They will make one long blast on the trumpets. When you hear that sound, have all the people give a loud shout. Then the walls of the city will fall. And the people will go straight into the city.' So the Israelites defeated that city. They completely destroyed every living thing in the city." Joshua 6:2-4, 20-21 ICB

When the *walls* are knocked down, the city is in danger. Just as when we lose our SELF-CONTROL which is our guard or protection, we are in danger of sin, i.e., getting angry, mad, saying something mean or disrespectful, etc.

Question #6: How can we protect our walls of SELF-CONTROL from falling down?

"'I will make this agreement with the people of Israel,' says the Lord. 'I will put my teachings in their minds. And I will write them on their hearts. I will be their God, and they will be my people.'" Jeremiah 31:33 ICB

Our walls of SELF-CONTROL will be protected when Jesus is in our hearts and His Word is in our minds.

> **Question #7:** Ask: Who can help us with SELF-CONTROL when we need it? Who can protect us from the sins caused by not having SELF-CONTROL? God can!

Explain: We can ask God to help us with our SELF-CONTROL. As the Bible says, He is always listening to our requests, and He takes joy when we bring our needs to Him.

ACTIVITY: *Walls of Protection*

- **For older Children:** If you have a hill in your yard or neighborhood take them outside to play *King of the Castle (Hill)*. You may need to find a local park area with a hill.
- **For younger Children:** Allow the children to build a fort with sheets, blankets, pillows, cushions, etc. You may need to build a fort for younger children.
- **For all ages:** Visit a fort in your area, or check out some books with pictures to help your child learn about forts and the walls that surrounded them.
- Talk about how the people inside the fort are protected by walls. Having SELF-CONTROL protects us.

Prayer: *Jesus, please keep me from losing self-control. Help me to control my words and actions. Please help me to remember that Your Word is a wall around me to protect me. I want to have self-control so I can be like You. Amen!*

DAY 3

PREP FOR MOM...

Today, we are going to talk about SELF-CONTROL—specifically with our words. When we do not have control over our words, they can be negative and often critical. We want to teach the children to control their words and make them uplifting to others and Jesus.

Familiarize yourself with the following verses:

"Lord, help me control my tongue. Help me be careful about what I say." Psalm 141:3 ICB

"God did not give us a spirit that makes us afraid. He gave us a spirit of power and love and self-control." 2 Timothy 1:7 ICB

ACTIVITY PROPS AND SUPPLIES:

- Construction paper (pink and red)
- Mini marshmallows
- Glue & scissors
- Ball jar
- Cotton balls

SCRIPT FOR MOM...

Read: "God did not give us a spirit that makes us afraid. He gave us a spirit of power and love and self-control." 2 Timothy 1:7 ICB

Question #1: According to our verse today, who has the ability to help us with our SELF-CONTROL? God does.

Today, we are going to talk about having SELF-CONTROL with our words. When we do not have control with our words, they can be unkind and unloving. But, God can help us have SELF-CONTROL with our words and use them to praise Him and encourage others.

Read: "Lord, help me control my tongue. Help me be careful about what I say." Psalm 141:3 ICB

Explain: The writer of this Psalm was asking God to protect his lips, to help him control his words. Did you know that we can pray and ask God to control our tongue and help us to be careful with our words? Let's do that right now. Note: Mommy pray with your child asking God to control our tongues and help us to praise Him and encourage others with our words. Read the verse below:

"My lips will praise You because Your loving-kindness is better than life." Psalm 63:3 NLV

Explain: When we control our tongue and direct our words to God, He is pleased. God loves it when we praise Him.

Question #2: What are some words that express our praise to God? Can you think of a song that brings praise to God? Let's sing it. Here is one:

This is the day, This is the day,
That the Lord has made, That the Lord has made
I will rejoice, I will rejoice and be glad in it, and be glad in it.
This is the day that Lord has made, I will rejoice and be glad in it.
This is the day, this is the day that the Lord has made.

"The mouth speaks of what the heart is full of." Luke 6:45 NLV

We have to work really hard to use SELF-CONTROL over our words, don't we? Maybe, a question we could ask ourselves before we speak is: Are the words I am about to speak pleasing to God and kind toward the person I am speaking to?

"Let us help each other to love others and to do good." Hebrews 10:24 NLV

"The mouth speaks of what the heart is full of." Luke 6:45 NLV

Explain: We are to love others and do good to others. If our heart is full of love, our words will express love. Our words, when controlled, can *help* others, *show love* to others and *encourage* others. Words can really make us smile and put a smile on the face of those around us.

Question #3: What are encouraging words we can use when talking to others? Can you think of a song that would encourage others? Let's sing it. Do you know *You are My Sunshine?*

ACTIVITY: *A Guarded Mouth* **or** *Lift Each Other Up*

- **For younger children:** Cut the pink paper into the shape of a mouth (oval). Fold in half. Then cut a tongue and glue it into the mouth. Next, draw circles where the marshmallows will go for the teeth. Glue the marshmallows on the circles. Talk about using SELF-CONTROL with our words. Write this verse on top of the mouth: "The mouth speaks of what the heart is full of."

- **For older children:** *Lift Each Other Up* jar: Decorate a large Ball jar. When the child speaks kind and uplifting words allow him to place a cotton ball in the jar. When the jar is full, take the family out for an ice cream. Explain that there are rewards for using SELF-CONTROL with our words!

Prayer: *Jesus, help me to have control over my words. I want to use my words to praise You and encourage others. Amen!*

DAY 4

PREP FOR MOM...

Re-read Galatians 5:22-23 and be prepared to talk about patience with your child. We will spend today talking about patience. To have patience, you must exercise SELF-CONTROL.

Familiarize yourself with the following verses:

"We ask you, brothers, to warn those who do not work. Encourage the people who are afraid. Help those who are weak. *Be patient* with every person." 1 Thessalonians 5:14 ICB

"Always be humble and gentle. *Be patient* and accept each other with love." Ephesians 4:2 ICB

ACTIVITY PROPS AND SUPPLIES:

Large open space for running

SCRIPT FOR MOM...

Today we are going to talk about patience. It was listed in the fruit of the Spirit we read about a couple of days ago.

> **Question #1:** Do you remember the verse on the fruit? Can you list the fruit?

Here we go: love, joy, peace, patience, kindness, goodness, faithfulness, gentleness, and self-control.

> **Question #2:** Do you know what it means to be patient? It is being willing to wait your turn without getting mad or frustrated.
>
> **Question #3:** Are there times when you have had to be patient? Tell me about it. Was it hard or easy to be patient when_____? Allow the child to tell you about the circumstance and how he felt.

Read: "We ask you, brothers, to warn those who do not work. Encourage the people who are afraid. Help those who are weak. Be *patient* with every person." 1 Thessalonians 5:14 ICB

Question #4: Who are we to be patient with? Just Mommy? Just our friends? No, EVERY PERSON!

Explain: Sometimes it might be hard to be patient with friends and family, especially if they are being mean, or taking a long time in the bathroom, or bugging you.

Discuss: Ephesians 4:2 "Always be humble and gentle. Be *patient* and accept each other with love." ICB

When we love people, we will exercise SELF-CONTROL and be patient with them. Sing this song about patience. (See: http://www.hisandhernandezmusic.com/store/patience)

Have patience, have patience
Don't be in such a hurry
When you get impatient, you only start to worry
Remember, remember that God is patient, too
And think of all the times when others have to wait for you

Question #5: What does it mean when mommy says, "You need to exercise patience?"

Explain: To exercise patience is to practice waiting with a good attitude.

Question #6: What are some activities or places we go where we have to wait our turn? Is it hard to wait? Is it hard to exercise SELF-CONTROL and be patient?

Remember our verse in 2 Timothy 1:7 that says, "God did not give us a spirit that makes us afraid. He gave us a spirit of power and love and self-control." (ICB) Explain: God enables us to have SELF-CONTROL and exercise patience in every circumstance.

ACTIVITY: *M&M Madness*

- Place one M&M in a container where your child can't see what is inside. Place the rest of the M&Ms in the other container.

- Explain that in this activity you are asking your child to have patience. If he does, he will have a great reward, but if not, the reward will be less.

- Tell your child he can have container 1 now (with 1 M&M) or if he waits _____ min or after dinner, he can have container 2 (with rest of M&Ms). After he chooses, discuss the possible outcomes and the choice that he made.

ACTIVITY: *Red Light- Green Light*

- Explain to your child that you are going to call out a color—Red or Green. When you say Green light, they can run. When you say red light, they immediately have to freeze and be patient while waiting for you to say green light again.

- Explain that you may say words that sound like "red" or "green." Encourage them to practice self-control and good listening skills by listening carefully. Afterward discuss what they had to be patient for? Was this easy, or hard?

Prayer: *Jesus, please help me to show others that I love them by being patient with them. When I am not patient, please show me and help me say I am sorry. Amen!*

DAY 5

PREP FOR MOM...

It has been a fun week looking at SELF-CONTROL and teaching the children how to have control *over their feelings and actions.* Today we are going to talk about a very special man who had control over His feelings and actions—Jesus. He set a wonderful example for us in exercising patience and using SELF-CONTROL.

Familiarize yourself with the following verses:

"Patience is better than strength. Controlling your temper is better than capturing a city." Proverbs 16:32 ICB

"A foolish person loses his temper. But a wise person controls his anger." Proverbs 29:11 ICB

"He was beaten down and punished. But he didn't say a word. He was like a lamb being led to be killed. He was quiet, as a sheep is quiet while its wool is being cut. He never opened his mouth." Isaiah 53:7 ICB

> *Jesus was patient in affliction (pain and suffering). He was not foolish (brainless, weak-minded) but he was wise in controlling his feelings. He used self-control over his emotions and in response to those who were hurting Him.*

ACTIVITY PROPS AND SUPPLIES:

- Bottle of soda (Coke, Sprite or any carbonated beverage)
- Towel and wet rag

SCRIPT FOR MOM...

Question #1: Over the past few days, what was your favorite part of the lesson on SELF-CONTROL?

Question #2: Can you tell me what SELF-CONTROL is?

We are going to talk about a very special man today. He set a wonderful example for us in exercising patience and using SELF-CONTROL. I am going to read a verse and let's see if you know who the writer is talking about.

"He was beaten down and punished. But he didn't say a word. He was like a lamb being led to be killed. He was quiet, as a sheep is quiet while its wool is being cut. He never opened his mouth." Isaiah 53:7 ICB

Question #3: Do you know who Isaiah was talking about in this verse? JESUS! That is right.

Explain: Jesus was beaten, stripped of his clothes, mocked and made fun of, and hung on a cross—yet he did not open his mouth. He used SELF-CONTROL. He did not say a word or try to repay them for their cruelty.

We are going to read a couple of verses on controlling your temper or anger.

"Patience is better than strength. Controlling your temper is better than capturing a city." Proverbs 16:32 ICB

"A foolish person loses his temper. But a wise person controls his anger." Proverbs 29:11 ICB

Explain: Jesus was patient in affliction (pain and suffering). He was not foolish (brainless, weak-minded) but he was wise in controlling his feelings. He used SELF-CONTROL over his emotions and in response to those who were hurting Him.

Question #4: If someone was treating you as cruelly as the Romans treated Jesus, would you be SELF-CONTROLLED?

Explain: When we are being picked on or treated badly by others, we should always use SELF-CONTROL and walk away from troublemakers.

ACTIVITY: *Out of Control*

- Take the children outside for this activity.

- Take a bottle of pop (carbonated beverage of choice) and shake it a lot. After a few seconds of shaking, remove the lid and watch the soda spew all over the place.

- Explain that Jesus even though he was shook and jostled, mistreated, beaten and spit upon, maintained His SELF-CONTROL.

- When we are shook and jostled and lose our SELF-CONTROL, we spew all over everyone around us. And what a mess!

- Remember these words: I use SELF-CONTROL. I think before I act or speak. I trust God to help me control my thoughts and actions.

Prayer: *Jesus, thank you for loving me so much that you went to the cross. You never got mad at those who were mean to You. You loved them even though they did not love You. Thank you for showing me how to control my emotions. Please make me more like You. Amen!*

FINDING

Peace

In this week's *Mommy and Me,* we will be talking about finding PEACE in the midst of *busy.* By definition, the word *peace* means freedom from disturbance.

In our everyday lives we are surrounded on every side by ongoing and unrelenting disturbances. So, according to the definition, *peace* is well out of our reach.

Jesus says in John 14:27, "Peace I leave with you; MY peace I give to you; not as the world gives do I give to you. Do not let your heart be troubled, nor let it be fearful." According to this verse, *peace* is not only available to us; it is intended for us! NASB

As Jesus spoke these words to His disciples, He highlighted that the PEACE He intended for them was much more than simply "freedom from disturbances." It was an inner settling, anchored in the reality of His Truth rather than in the reality of their circumstances.

Helping our children to find PEACE in the midst of busy requires giving them an anchor and showing them how to work it.

That anchor is Truth. Learning to work that anchor is our mission for the next 5 days.

Ready! Set! Find PEACE!

DAY 1

PREP FOR MOM...

Read: The story of Jehoshaphat in 2 Chronicles 20:1-30.

Familiarize yourself with the following verses for references if needed:

- Psalm 29. This passage was written as a celebration of God's glory, as shown through His ultimate power, highlighting how He reveals Himself through nature and how He blesses His people.
- Isaiah 26:1-9. This passage was written as a celebration of God's all consuming power and faithful protection of His people.

Go ahead and mark these passages in your Bible with a sticky note or slip of paper so that they're easy to get to. You'll come back to these verses each day and later you will be using Psalm 29:11 and Isaiah 26:3 with your child.

When big, hard, hurtful things happen that we cannot control they can take away our peace.

For today's time, summarize the story of Jehoshaphat in 2 Chronicles 20:1-30.

- Be sure to point out that Jehoshaphat was a *righteous* king of Judah (Judah endured a total of 20 kings before the exile.)
- Only 7 of them were righteous who sought after God, tore down idol worship, organized the teaching of God's law in all the cities of his kingdom, and consequently enjoyed an abundance of God's blessing.

ACTIVITY PROPS AND SUPPLIES:

- Paper, crayons, markers, etc. for drawing pictures
- Streamers, balloons, trophies, etc. for decorating (optional)

SCRIPT FOR MOM...

Sometimes life gets too busy—too many places to be, too many nights away from home, too many things to do. Sometimes hard things happen (we fall down and get hurt badly, we lose a big game, a grandparent gets very sick). Sometimes things just get down right hurtful (a pet runs away or dies, friends are mean, we get into a car wreck, parents get divorced). When things like this happen, we might start feeling tired, worried, lonely, sad, nervous, or scared. When big, hard, hurtful things happen that we cannot control, they can take away our PEACE.

- King Jehoshaphat (king of Judah) knew about chaos. He found himself right in the middle of it in 2 Chronicles 20.

- Tell the story: A big mean army had come to fight with King Jehoshaphat and his people, and the King was scared. He yelled to the Lord "What do we do?" The Lord replied simply, "PRAISE Me. And, I'll take care of all your trouble."

- Read verses 20-22 and see how King Jehoshaphat gathered all his people and did exactly what the Lord had said. They stood together on the battlefield and, as one big group, started singing and PRAISING God for being so awesome! (That would have been really cool to see and hear, don't you think!)

- As soon as God heard Judah's praises, He began taking care of their trouble.

- First, He sent a new army to fight Jehoshaphat's enemies so Judah wouldn't have to fight them.

- Then, God confused Jehoshaphat's enemies so they ended up destroying each other.

- Judah was saved.

- God rescued King Jehoshaphat and Judah from their troubles and gave them PEACE because they PRAISED Him!

Explain: Whenever troubles threaten us, we should do the same thing King Jehoshaphat did. We should PRAISE God!! And when we do, God will do for us the same thing he did for Judah. He will rescue us and give us PEACE.

Question #1: What are some things that make God the absolute most wonderful, amazing, fantastic, awesome One ever? Take a little while to answer this question. (Be sure to point out how happy our heart feels when you talk about these things.)

ACTIVITY:

- Draw pictures celebrating a few of your favorite awesome things about God and then hang the pictures in a special place in your house (on the fireplace, on the wall in the hall).

- If you like, decorate the area around your pictures with streamers, trophies, balloons, etc. to show even more celebration of how special God is!

Prayer: *Dear God, I am so thankful that You are big and awesome! Help me to always remember who You are when hard and hurtful things happen. When trouble comes, I will not fear. I'll PRAISE instead. Amen!*

DAY 2

PREP FOR MOM...

Familiarize yourself with the following verses:

Read Psalm 55. In these verses, David had been painfully betrayed by a very close friend. He was expressing his pain to God in anguish of his own soul, anger at his friend's betrayal, and assurance of God's attentiveness and redemption in the matter. Make note of David's hurts/ big heavy feelings and how he turned them (cast his cares) over to God.

"Cast all your anxiety on him because he cares for you." 1 Peter 5:7

ACTIVITY PROPS AND SUPPLIES:

- A backpack or tote bag
- A pile of bricks (Any heavy objects that would represent our big heavy feelings)
- A popsicle (To represent God's big wonderful love)

Choose a Point A and a Point B with a short distance in between. Your child will put the bricks in the backpack and try to carry it from Point A to Point B while also eating a popsicle. Note: It might be best to do this activity outside.

SCRIPT FOR MOM...

E is for Express and Enjoy!

Begin with the activity. This activity will be your main lesson today and will require the most time.

Activity: Ask the children to take a look at this pile of bricks. (Any chosen heavy object)

> **Question #1:** How hard do you think it would be to carry these bricks from here (Point A) to there (Point B)?

Have each child hold 1 brick. Ask them to walk around the room carrying the brick.

- Talk about how heavy the brick is and how it feels to hold it and carry it.
- What about 2 bricks? Ask them to walk around the room carrying the bricks. Talk about how much heavier and more awkward it is to carry 2 bricks.

Say to the children: Now I have a challenge for you:

- First, put all the bricks in the backpack and carry it full of bricks from Point A to Point B while also eating this popsicle! The rule for this activity is that you cannot stop doing one to do the other. You have to do both at the same time!
- Talk about how very heavy the backpack of bricks is and how yummy the Popsicle is, but how hard it is to enjoy the popsicle because you are carrying the bag of bricks.
- Explain that you're missing out enjoying the goodness of the popsicle because it's melting while you're struggling to carry the bag of bricks. Make note, it's hard enough to just pick up the bag, much less walk and eat a Popsicle, too!

Now let's stop a minute and change things up. One by one, take the bricks out of the bag and throw them away as far as you can—without hitting a sibling.

- Hold the popsicle for him and cheer for your child as he throws the bricks as hard and as far as he can. Explain that he wants them as far away as possible in order not to have to worry with them anymore.

> *"Cast all your anxiety on him because he cares for you."* 1 Peter 5:7

- When the bricks are all thrown, give your child the popsicle with lots of celebration.
- Sit down to rest and talk about how good the popsicle is and how it is easier to enjoy it without trying to carry the load of bricks at the same time.

Explain: When big, hard, hurtful things happen in our lives, they are like our backpack full of bricks—heavy and hard to carry around inside of us. Also, they make it hard for us to enjoy God's love and PEACE. Because God knew life could be hard for us, He made a plan for what we should do with our 'bag of bricks' feelings.

- The Bible tells us to "cast our cares" on God. (Psalm 55:22 and 1 Peter 5:7)

- The word "cast" in the verse means to throw our cares at God, not to be taken back. To throw our cares or feelings means we EXPRESS them—we get them out.

- With our big heavy feelings gone, there's nothing to weigh us down or distract us. We can then hold on to God's big wonderful love (the popsicle!) and ENJOY the sweetness of it! We stand straighter, step lighter, rest easier, and have His PEACE.

King David wrote (in Psalms 55) about a time when one of his closest friends had betrayed (hurt) him. (Betray means to fail or desert especially in time of need.) Because David's feelings were hurt and his life was in danger, he was telling God all about it. Without reading the entire chapter, point out for the children some of David's 'bag of bricks' feelings.

Explain how he threw these feelings at God, believing God loved him and would rescue him. Note: If your children are older, you might want to have them read through the chapter and write down some of David's 'bag of bricks' feelings.

Whenever troubles threaten us, we should be like King David and EXPRESS our big heavy feelings to God and in exchange ENJOY His big wonderful love and PEACE.

Prayer: *Dear God, Your love is the best thing in the whole world! Help me remember to throw my hurt feelings on You and enjoy Your love. I want to EXPRESS them and ENJOY You—and carry on! Amen!*

DAY 3

PREP FOR MOM...

Familiarize yourself with the following verses:

Read Exodus 14. The Israelites had been rescued from slavery in Egypt. They were ecstatically on their way to a new home and free life in a beautiful land God had made just for them. Their expectations were quickly challenged and their faith tested. Note, how quickly and powerfully God swooped in to keep them safe and keep His promise!

ACTIVITY PROPS AND SUPPLIES:

- Index cards
- Flashlight (To represent the pillar of cloud/fire)
- Toy soldiers (To represent Egyptians/Israelites)

SCRIPT FOR MOM...

A is for Assurance

Remind your child that when we get rid of our 'bag of bricks' feelings, it's easier to see that God is still with us, loves us and is taking care of us. Today we are going to look at the story of the children of Israel who were having a very hard time as slaves in Egypt. We will see how God loved them, protected and provided for them.

Question #1: What is a slave? Definition: A person who is the legal property of another and is forced to obey them.

Often in hard times, God says and does special things to remind us of His love for us. He did just this for the children of Israel who were *slaves* in Egypt.

Question #2: What are some ways God shows His love for us? Help the children list a few.

Explain: When God does these things for us, we have absolute ASSURANCE of His presence (being with us) and His protection (taking care of us). (Assurance is being certain.)

Briefly tell the story from Exodus 14. Point out the following:

- Moses and the Israelites got to see God's presence and protection in a very exciting way!
- The Israelites were led out of Egypt by God's very special friend, Moses.
- Suddenly they found themselves stuck between a deep sea that they couldn't cross and the mean king's army that they couldn't outrun. In this very chaotic moment, God gave the Israelites the ASSURANCE He knew they needed.
- Using Moses as His messenger, God said something very special! "But Moses answered, 'Don't be afraid! Stand still and see the Lord save you today. You will never see these Egyptians again after today. You will only need to remain calm. The Lord will fight for you.'" Exodus 14:13-14 (ICB)
- God did something very special. "The angel of God usually traveled in front of Israel's army. Now the angel of God moved behind them. Also, the pillar of cloud moved from in front of the people and stood behind them. So the cloud came between the Egyptians and the people of Israel. The cloud made it dark for the Egyptians. But it gave light to the Israelites. So the cloud kept the two armies apart all night." Exodus 14:19-20 (ICB)

When trouble surrounds us, we can have absolute ASSURANCE of God's presence and protection, too! All we have to do is remember His Word, watch for His Work and experience His Peace.

...Isn't that amazing!?! God gave His people plenty of ASSURANCE that He was with them and taking good care of them...all the time! Along with that assurance came a great PEACE. When trouble surrounds us, we can have absolute ASSURANCE of God's presence and protection, too! All we have to do is remember His Word, watch for His Work and experience His PEACE.

ACTIVITY:

- Turn off all the lights in the room and close the blinds. Lay a flashlight on a TV tray or small table in the middle of the room. Help your child set up the toy soldiers or dolls somewhere behind the dark end of the flashlight (so they're in the dark). You and your child should position yourselves in the light of the flashlight.

- Talk about what it would have been like to be an Israelite in Exodus 14! Act out crossing the Red Sea, wondering what the soldiers were doing, remembering God's Word to them from verses 13-14, trusting Him, experiencing freedom, being awed by His miracles, etc.

- Next, switch places with the soldiers! Sit together in the dark and talk about what it would have been like to be an Egyptian in Exodus 14! Ugh!

Look up a couple of verses that tell us that God is always with us/ will never leave us. Write these verses on index cards. Note: If you have small children, you may want to have the cards done ahead of time.

- Talk about the promises you wrote on index cards. Tell your child how true these promises are!

- Share an age appropriate story about a troubling time when God gave you ASSURANCE of His presence and protection.

Prayer: *Dear God, the Bible says You are with me ALL the time, and I believe it! Help me to learn and love Your Word! Help me see and believe your Work! Help me remember that Your Word and Work will give me the assurance and PEACE I need!! Amen!*

PREP FOR MOM...

Familiarize yourself with the following verses:

Exodus 17:8-16. In these verses, the Israelites were facing many different challenges on their way to the Promised Land. These troubles were strengthening their faith and helping them learn to live well with God and each other.

1 Corinthians 12:12-27. Paul is writing about the many different parts of the body of Christ— each being unique and valuable. He encourages believers to relate to each other with mutual honor and respect and to share intentionally in each other's joys and sufferings.

ACTIVITY PROPS AND SUPPLIES:

- Materials for making a card
- Ingredients for baking cookies or preparing a meal
- Flowers

SCRIPT FOR MOM...

C is for Care

So far we've learned that when trouble comes, we should...

- Give God PRAISE (Like King Jehoshaphat and Judah).
- EXPRESS our big heavy feelings and ENJOY God's big wonderful love (Like King David).
- Look to God's words and works for the ASSURANCE of His presence, power and PEACE. (Like Moses and the Israelites).

Explain: PRAISING God, EXPRESSING our heavy feelings, ENJOYING God's love and living in ASSURANCE of His presence, power and PEACE helps us to always trust Him and live free of fear and worry.

When we do these things, we see more and more of God and less and less of our troubles. It also helps us to show those around us who are dealing with troubles the love and care of God. As God CARES for us, He wants us to CARE for others!

The story of Aaron and Hur in Exodus 17 gives us a great visual of CARING for one another. Note: The rescued Israelites are now on their way from Egypt to Canaan—the land God had promised them.

"At Rephidim the Amalekites came and fought the Israelites. So Moses said to Joshua, "Choose some men and go and fight the Amalekites. Tomorrow I will stand on the top of the hill. I will hold the stick God gave me to carry." Joshua obeyed Moses and went to fight the Amalekites. At the same time Moses, Aaron and Hur went to the top of the hill. As long as Moses held his hands up, the Israelites would win the fight. But when Moses put his hands down, the Amalekites would win. Later, Moses' arms became tired. So the men put a large rock under Moses, and he sat on it. Then Aaron and Hur held up Moses' hands. Aaron was on one side of Moses, and Hur was on the other side. They held his hands up like this until the sun went down. So Joshua defeated the Amalekites in this battle." Exodus 17: 8-13 ICB

Question #1: What trouble did Moses have?

Question #2: How did Aaron and Hur CARE for Moses?

Isn't that awesome!?! Moses began to get tired. Aaron and Hur shared their strength and with their help, Moses was able to survive his troubles. God once again destroyed Israel's enemies!

God wants to use us to take CARE of others just like He takes CARE of us!

"God did this so that our body (the church) would not be divided. God wanted the different parts to CARE the same for each other. If one part of the body suffers, then all the other parts suffer with it. Or if one part of our body is honored, then all the other parts share its honor. All of you together are the body of Christ. Each one of you is a part of that body." 1 Corinthians 12:25 ICB

ACTIVITY:

- Think of someone you know who is dealing with sadness, difficulty, illness, etc. They might be weary and tired and could use some encouragement.

> **Question #3:** How can we help or encourage _____? If possible, do what your children suggest as ways to care for and encourage your hurting family, friends or neighbors.

ADDITIONAL IDEAS:

- Have the children create a fun and encouraging card to give them. Mail it or deliver it with a plate of cookies or flowers.

- Perhaps you could help them with chores—raking their leaves or cleaning their house.

- Be available to watch their children while they run errands.

- Take them a meal or a special dessert prepared by you and your children.

- Whatever you decide to do, remember, you are showing that you CARE in order to remind others that God CARES for them!! Your family and those you help will see God more and more and troubles less and less! What a happy surprise for everyone!

Prayer: *Dear God, Thank you for taking care of me. Use me to encourage someone who is sad, tired or lonely! Help me to remember to show Your loving CARE to others. What You give me, I'll share. Amen!*

DAY 5

PREP FOR MOM...

Familiarize yourself with the following verses…

Read Ephesians 3. Paul was writing to the Gentile Christians about the mystery of Christ and God's grace which drew the Gentiles into the fellowship and blessing of God's family. This made them feel fully loved as chosen heirs of His salvation and glory!

In preparation for this week, you might want to be searching the Bible for God's promises. Write the promises you find on index cards for your family *Promise Box* to be made today.

SCRIPT FOR MOM...

E is for Expect

After we give God PRAISE, EXPRESS our big heavy problems, ENJOY His big wonderful love, find ASSURANCE of His presence, protection and PEACE, and show His loving CARE to others, there is only one thing left for us to do!

EXPECT God to do something wonderful…in the spirit of Ephesians 3:20-21. Read aloud: "With God's power working in us, God can do much, much more than anything we can ask or think of. To him be glory in the church and in Christ Jesus for all time, forever and ever. Amen." (ICB) These verses are some of the best in the whole Bible at simply showing us how big and awesome our God is.

- Explain that these verses are a promise from God.
- The Bible is full of God's promises.
- One of God's many names is Promise Keeper.
- He always keeps His word. Over and over again in the Bible, we see where God made a promise and kept His Word.

Examples: Abraham, Moses and Noah (Choose one or two and in simple terms tell of the promise God made to each and how He kept His promise.)

Explain: We have no reason to doubt God and every reason to trust Him! With His PEACE in our hearts, we can wait and watch to see how well things will turn out. We can trust the heart of our most loving and most powerful God!

Note: There is no specific Activity planned for today. Instead you have an assignment:

Begin a collection of God's promises!!

- You might borrow or buy a book that lists them. Thomas Nelson has several good books of God's promises for people of different ages and stages!

- You might Google a list of them. A website named 365promises.com lists a promise from God for each day of the year!

- You might ask around for them. Family and friends who love Jesus would be happy to tell you the promises of God that have become very special to them.

- However you choose to go about it, begin gathering the specific promises of God.

- As you get each one, look it up in your Bible, write it on an index card, read it out loud, then practice believing that promise by simply saying to God, "I believe Your promise!"

- Place your promise cards in a family *Promise Box* that has been made and decorated by your children.

You and your family may not fully understand or even feel that you need the promises you are reading at this time, but there may come a day, at some point in your lives, when those exact words will be the thing that rescues you from some kind of trouble.

Explain to the children that if God's promises are tucked away in our heart, highlighted in our Bible, or written on cards in our family *Promise Box*, they'll be ready to go. All you'll have to do is pull them out and read them over and over and over again.

In conclusion, busyness, trouble and heartache are a part of life. They just are. But they don't have to steal our PEACE.

And they won't, when we're held by the Truth and that Truth is that...

God loves us and is always doing good for us! Based on that, I can cooperate with Him and trust Him, no matter what happens, and then wait to see how well things turn out!

- This Truth is our ANCHOR.
- All we have to do to make it work is...Give God PRAISE!
- EXPRESS to Him our big heavy feelings and in return ENJOY His big wonderful love!
- Look to His Word and works to find the ASSURANCE of His presence, protection and PEACE!
- Show God's loving CARE to others!
- EXPECT God to do something wonderful!!
- Then you will have PEACE in the midst of chaos!!

Prayer: *Dear God, You always keep Your promises! You love me and are always doing good for me! I can trust Your heart. Thank You for teaching me* TRUTH *and showing me how to have* PEACE. *Amen!*

The Power of the

Tongue

In this week's *Mommy and Me,* we will be talking about the TONGUE. It is such a small part of the human body, yet it wields so much power! We will take a look at what God has to say about the TONGUE and apply His instructions to the use of our words.

Our TONGUE can be used to lift others up or tear them down. The words we speak have the power of life or death. We can show love and appreciation or express dislike and even hatred with our TONGUE.

> *Our tongue can be used to lift others up or tear them down. The words we speak have the power of life or death.*

There are many verses in God's Word on the TONGUE. One of the most powerful says that "out of the heart the mouth speaks." Therefore, we will look at verses on the heart. Often what is in our hearts comes out through our mouths.

Ready! Set! The power of the TONGUE!

DAY 1

PREP FOR MOM...

Familiarize yourself with the following verses:

"Death and life are in the power of the TONGUE, and those who love it will eat its fruit." Proverbs 18:21 NASB

"If anyone thinks himself to be religious, and yet does not bridle his TONGUE but deceives his own heart, this man's religion is worthless." James 1:26 NASB

"Death and life are in the power of the tongue, and those who love it will eat its fruit." Proverbs 18:21 NASB

Explain that according to these verses, our TONGUES are very powerful! This week you will want to convey to your children that the words they say really do matter and can have an impact on others—for good or bad.

ACTIVITY PROPS AND SUPPLIES:

- Index cards
- Black marker
- Tape

SCRIPT FOR MOM...

The Bible says this about the TONGUE: "Death and life are in the power of the TONGUE, and those who love it will eat its fruits." Proverbs 18:21 NASB

Facts about the human TONGUE: (The facts listed may only be understood by older children—you may need to simplify for younger children.)

- The TONGUE is a muscular organ in the mouth. It is of importance in the digestive system and is the primary organ of taste.

- The TONGUE'S upper surface is covered in taste buds. It is sensitive and kept moist by saliva. It is full of nerves and blood vessels.

- The TONGUE serves as a natural means of cleaning the teeth. A major function of the tongue is the enabling of speech in humans.

- There are two groups of muscles of the TONGUE. The four intrinsic muscles alter the shape of the tongue and are not attached to bone. The four paired extrinsic muscles change the position of the tongue and are anchored to bone.

Perhaps you thought that the TONGUE was the smallest of all the human organs—it's not! Actually, the pineal gland is considered to be the smallest organ in the human body. It is located deep inside the brain. (Organ: A part of a person that is specialized to perform a particular function) Although the tongue is not the smallest organ in the human body, it is a small organ that can do a large amount of damage.

Read: "If anyone thinks himself to be religious, and yet does not bridle (control) his TONGUE but deceives his own heart, this man's religion is worthless." James 1:26 NASB

Explain how a bridle is used to control a horse. Sometimes our TONGUES can be loose and speak words that they shouldn't. We are to control our tongues like a bridle controls a horse. Unbridled TONGUES can say hurtful things.

> **Question #1:** Has there ever been a time when someone *said* something to you that made you feel really good? For example: Maybe someone (A teacher or mommy or daddy) complimented you or said they were so glad to see you. Give each child an opportunity to answer.
>
> **Question #2:** Did you know that you can use your words to bring joy and happiness to others? God's Word says, "An anxious heart weighs a man down, but a kind word cheers him up." Proverbs 12:25 NIV
>
> **Question #3:** What are some ways you can use your words to make others happy and feel good?

Example of a way my son used his words to make his Mimi feel good: Recently, while my husband and I were out of town, my sweet in-laws took on the task of caring for our toddler.

One night he was watching a movie while my mother-in-law was in the adjoining room preparing for bedtime. As she walked out in her modest nightgown, he exclaimed, "Mimi, you look FANTASTIC!" We chuckled as she relayed the story to us the next day and wondered where he learned the phrase. He made his Mimi feel good!

ACTIVITY:

- Ask your child how he or she might use words to lift up and encourage others today. How might you encourage your mommy or daddy? Your brother or sister?

- Make a list of "feel good" or "life giving" words. Using the list, write each word on an index card.

- Allow the children to tape or place the cards around the house in various locations. Whenever anyone in the family enters a room where a card was left, he has to use the "feel good" or "life giving" word found on the card and to say something kind about one of the other family members.

- **Parents:** Practice saying life-giving words to your children this week. Remember one of the best ways that they can learn is by repeating what they hear from you!

Prayer: *Dear God, thank you for teaching me about words and my* TONGUE *from the Bible. Thank you for giving me a way to bless others by what I say. Help me to honor You, my family, and my friends with my words today. Amen!*

DAY 2

PREP FOR MOM...

Familiarize yourself with the verses below:

Verse from yesterday:

"Death and life are in the power of the TONGUE, and those who love it will eat its fruit." Proverbs 18:21 NASB

Verse for today:

"The mouth of the righteous is a fountain of life…" Proverbs 10:11 NASB

> *Do not underestimate the power of life-giving words! You can make someone's day with an encouraging word.*

Be prepared to give examples of ways others have encouraged and blessed you with their words. Share opportunities you have had to bless and encourage others with "life giving" words.

ACTIVITY PROPS AND SUPPLIES:

- Blank note cards
- Thank you note cards
- Stamps
- Dry-erase marker

SCRIPT FOR MOM...

Talk about yesterday's lesson and the importance of words and how we can use them to bless others. Ask your child how he or she used the "life giving" word cards to bless or encourage a family member. **For younger children:** Help them hide the cards and then later go searching for them. As you find each card, read the word and ask them to say something nice about daddy, mommy, sister or brother using the word on the card.

Question #1: Do you remember our verse from yesterday?

"Death and life are in the power of the TONGUE, and those who love it will eat its fruit." Proverbs 18:21 NASB

Question #2: How can life and death be in the TONGUE? We can crush someone's spirit by saying unkind, mean and hurtful words or we can make him happy by saying kind and "life giving" words to him.

Our verse today says, "The mouth of the righteous is a fountain of life…" Proverbs 10:11 NASB

Question #3: What flows from a fountain? Answer: Water. Water refreshes us, doesn't it?

When we are tired, hot, and thirsty, water can refresh and energize us. Our words are to flow from us as refreshment to those who hear them. Our words should be used to make others feel better.

Do not underestimate the power of life-giving words! You can make someone's day with an encouraging word—not only family but others like friends, teachers, the mail carrier, etc.

Question #4: Can you think of ways, other than speaking, that we can use our words to lift others up? Wait for the children to answer then list the ideas below:

ACTIVITY:

Take a moment today to use your words to bless others by doing one of the examples below (or one your child thought of!):

- Send a card in the mail to a friend who needs encouragement.
- Give a thank you note to your waiter at your meal out today.
- Pray for a friend that is going through a hard time.

- Write a sweet note and put it in your sibling's lunchbox before school.

- Write a letter to your parents thanking them for the way they care for you.

- Write on your sibling's or parent's mirror (with a dry-erase marker) scripture or the words YOU ARE SPECIAL to encourage them.

- Leave a thank you note in your mailbox for your mail-carrier. (Any service person)

Prayer: *Dear God, please show me today how I can bless others with a written word. Show me one person who needs encouragement from You. Thank you for using me to love others. Amen!*

PREP FOR MOM...

So far, we have talked about the positive words that we can speak and write to others. Today we will see that just as our words can bring healing, they can also tear others down.

Familiarize yourself with these verses:

"Reckless words pierce like a sword, but the TONGUE of the wise brings healing." Proverbs 12:18 NIV

God hears our every word. Words that hurt others also hurt God.

"A gentle TONGUE is a tree of life, but perverseness in it breaks the spirit." Proverbs 15:4 ESV

ACTIVITY PROPS AND SUPPLIES:

- An inexpensive tube of toothpaste for each child
- Paper plates
- Paper towels for clean up

SCRIPT FOR MOM...

Today we will see that just as our words can bring others healing, they can also tear them down.

Read: "A gentle TONGUE is a tree of life, but perverseness in it breaks the spirit."
Proverbs 15:4 ESV

"Reckless words pierce like a sword, but the TONGUE of the wise brings healing."
Proverbs 12:18 NIV

Ask the children to help you make a list of hurtful words. Example: Calling someone stupid, dumb, nerd, ugly, baby, etc.

Did you know God hears our every word. Words that hurt others also hurts God.

You might have heard other children say, "Sticks and stones may break my bones but words will never hurt me."

Question #1: Is this really true? No! Words are hurtful.

Question #2: Once you say something hurtful to someone, can you get your words back? No! The damage (hurt) has already been inflicted.

Question #3: You cannot get your hurtful words back, but what can you do to make up for the hurt you caused mommy, daddy, sister, brother or a friend? You can apologize and ask the person you hurt and God to forgive you.

Question #4: Do you think that what you say matters to God? Yes! God has much to say about your TONGUE and your words in the Bible. He says that He wants you to love others through your words, not tear them down or hurt them. Our words matter.

For the activity today, we are going to use a tube of toothpaste to illustrate how once the hurtful words are out of our mouths we cannot get them back.

ACTIVITY:

- Go to this link: (YouTube, Bruners Explain Family Nights https://www.youtube.com/watch?v=4k1JDIFH6cQ). Give each child a tube of toothpaste and a paper plate. Instruct him that it is a race to see who can squeeze the paste out the fastest. If you have one child, you could use a timer to see how fast he can squeeze it out onto the plate. The next step is to see who can get the paste back in the tube first. In this illustration, the paste resembles our words. Once we say them, they cannot be taken back and the impact has been made.

- Think about the words that you have said to others (words you cannot get back) over the past twenty-four hours. Did you say anything that might have hurt their feelings or discouraged them?

- God's Word says, "Do not let any unwholesome talk come out of your mouths, but only what is helpful for building others up according to their needs, that it may benefit those who listen" Ephesians 4:29 NIV. The good news is that if you have said something harmful, God forgives when you ask him! Also, God offers you the chance to go to that person and ask him to forgive you. Is there someone you need to ask forgiveness from today?

Prayer: *"May the words of my mouth and the meditation of my heart be pleasing to You, O Lord, my Rock and my Redeemer" (Psalm 19:14 NLT). God, I want to honor You and encourage others with my words. Amen!*

DAY 4

PREP FOR MOM...

> *"Do all things without grumbling or disputing." Philippians 2:14 ESV*

In yesterday's lesson, we talked about how our words can be used positively or negatively. Today we want the children to see that just as our words can be used in harming others, another negative use of our words is when we complain, grumble, or argue.

Familiarize yourself with the following verses and the definitions of the following words:

"Do all things without grumbling or disputing." Philippians 2:14 ESV

In other words...

"Do everything readily and cheerfully – no bickering, no second-guessing allowed!" Philippians 2:14 The Message

Words defined:

- Grumble: To mutter (to utter words with a low voice) in discontent
- Complain: To express grief, pain or discontentment
- Argue: To disagree in words

ACTIVITY PROPS AND SUPPLIES:

- Small to medium ball jar per child (If child is too young for glass, use plastic container.)
- Bag of dry beans
- Markers or acrylic paint
- Throw-away plastic tablecloth to protect furniture or counter

SCRIPT FOR MOM...

Just as our words can be used to harm others, another negative use of our words is when we complain, grumble, or argue.

Question #1: What does it mean to grumble or complain? Use the definitions given to help the children understand the negative meaning of these words: Grumble, complain and argue.

In the Bible, three of Jesus' apostles, Paul, James, and Peter, wrote warning the people not to grumble or complain. They said "don't grumble" and "stop grumbling."

Question #2: What is your reaction when mommy, daddy or your teacher asks you to pick up your things (toys, clothes, backpack, etc.) or to do your chores?

Question #3: Do you ever complain about something you do not enjoy doing?

Question #4: Does God hear our grumbling, complaining or arguing with others? Yes, He does!

This is what He says about it: "Do all things without grumbling or disputing." Philippians 2:14 ESV

God says "Do ALL things without grumbling or complaining." That means we are not to grumble or complain about anything we are asked to do.

Read:

"He who guards his lips guards his life." Proverbs 13:3a NIV

"A wise man's heart guides his mouth." Proverbs 16:23a NIV

Explain: Through the help of the Holy Spirit, God can daily transform our speech and tone. Instead of talking about how hot it is outside, try talking about what a beautiful day it is. As we use our language to thank the Lord, compliment others, encourage friends, and praise God, it leaves less "room" for the grumbling, complaining, arguing, and tearing others down.

Say: Let's be mindful today of every word we speak, especially in the difficult moments of our day. Think about the words you are going to say *before* you say them. This is one way to "guard your mouth" and replace words of grumbling with words of cheer!

ACTIVITY:

- Give each child a *Ball* jar. (They can decorate their jar with markers or paint)

- Explain that for the next two weeks every time they are asked to do something by mommy, daddy or a sibling and do not grumble or complain, they can place a bean in their jar.

- At the end of the two weeks, the child with the most beans gets a treat. (A trip to the yogurt store or to the bookstore for a new book)

- If the other children want an opportunity to do better and win a treat, start over and go for another two weeks.

Prayer: *Thank you, Lord, for teaching me today about my mouth. "Set a guard over my mouth, O Lord, over my mouth; keep watch over the door of my lips!" (Psalm 141:3 NIV) Help me not to grumble and complain when I am asked to do something I do not want to do. Amen!*

DAY 5

PREP FOR MOM...

This week we have talked about how small the TONGUE is— yet it wields a great deal of power! Be prepared to review the week with the children. See what verses they can remember.

"Death and life are in the power of the TONGUE, and those who love it will eat its fruit." Proverbs 18:21 NASB

You have taught the children that the words they say really do matter and can have an impact on others—for good or bad. You made a list of "life giving" words and helped the children find ways to use them to bless and encourage others.

As God's children, we are to use our words to praise and honor Him.

You discussed negative hurtful words and the pain they can cause. You told the children that just as our words can be used to harm others, another negative use of our words is when we complain, grumble, or argue.

Check everyone's jars since yesterday and see how they are doing with not complaining or grumbling when asked to do something.

ACTIVITY PROPS AND SUPPLIES:

- Favorite praise and worship CD
- i-Pad to play YouTube music worship video

SCRIPT FOR MOM...

Using the reminders from above, review this week's devotional with the children. Ask questions such as:

Question #1: Who can tell me what we talked about this week?

Question #2: What did we say about the TONGUE? About our words?

Today we are going to talk about our TONGUE and how we can use our mouth and our words to bless God. For younger children: You may want to summarize the following verses:

Read: "Now if we put the bits into the horses' mouths so that they will obey us, we direct their entire body as well. Look at the ships also, though they are so great and are driven by strong winds, are still directed by a very small rudder wherever the inclination of the pilot desires. So also the TONGUE is a small part of the body, and *yet* it boasts of great things. But no one can tame the TONGUE; *it is* a restless evil *and* full of deadly poison. With it we bless *our* Lord and Father, and with it we curse men, who have been made in the likeness of God; from the same mouth come *both* blessing and cursing. My brethren, these things ought not to be this way." James 3:3-10 NASB

Focus special attention on the verse, "With it we bless our Lord and Father...

Question #4: Did you know we are able to bless *God* with our words? Can we bring glory to Him through what we say? Discuss ways we can bless God and bring Him glory with our words.

Those who have Jesus living in their hearts are called followers of Christ. As His children, we can use our words to praise and honor Him. Try it! Speak verses out loud that praise God and reveal His names, His character, and His virtues. Examples of verses that praise and bless the Lord:

"I will bless the Lord at all times; his praise shall continually be in my mouth."
Psalm 34:1 NASB

"For great is the LORD and greatly to be praised; He is to be feared above all gods."
Psalm 96:4 NASB

Another way to use your words to bless the Lord is through song. Ask the children: Do you have a favorite song that you would like to praise the Lord with today?

ACTIVITY:

- Turn on your favorite praise CD or K-Love radio and worship the Lord with your words of praise! Allow the children to dance around the house along with the music.
- For small children you may want to choose songs suited for their age.

Prayer: *Dear God, thank you for creating my mouth. Give me a heart and tongue that bless You and others. May this be true of me: "My mouth is filled with Your praise and with Your glory all the day." Amen!* Psalm 71:8 ESV

Note: Sweet fellow mama, my prayer is that we become mothers of praise and that our children hear the Excellencies of the Lord spilling from our mouths and filling our homes. He is worthy!

"I will sing of the steadfast love of the LORD, forever; with my mouth I will make known your faithfulness *to all generations*." Psalm 89:1 ESV

CHOOSING TO BE

Content

In this week's *Mommy and Me*, we will be talking about CONTENTMENT. Webster defines contentment as the state of being contented; satisfaction, not desiring more than one has; satisfied; resigned to circumstances, assenting, satisfied with things as they are.

We live in a world where social media is constantly an open door to compare ourselves to others' best. It's not that we compare our *normal* to others' *normal*; we often compare our *normal* to others' best. It is hard to be satisfied, content and not desire more than what we have.

> *"I have learned the secret of being content in any and every situation, whether well fed or hungry, whether living in plenty or in want. I can do all this through him who gives me strength."*
> Philippians 4:12-13 NIV

Our children are watching, and we have a *choice* as to how we respond to the pull of the world. This is an area in our children's lives where more is "caught than taught." Mommy, remember, CONTENTMENT is not a feeling. It is a *choice*.

Discontentment is something that we ALL face at some point in our lives. How we deal with it will determine the level of peace and satisfaction in our hearts and in our homes.

What are you teaching your children about CONTENTMENT? Paul reminds us that we are to be content in all circumstances. "I know what it is to be in need, and I know what it is to have plenty. I have *learned the secret of being content in any and every situation*, whether well fed or hungry, whether living in plenty or in want. I can do all this through him who gives me strength." Philippians 4:12-13 NIV

This week, we will be teaching our children four basic principles for CONTENTMENT:

- To choose not to focus on what I don't have, but to be grateful for what God has given me.

- To choose not to focus on what others have.

- To choose to be generous with what I have.

- To choose contagious CONTENTMENT.

Ready! Set! Be CONTENT!

DAY 1

PREP FOR MOM...

This week we are teaching on CONTENTMENT. It is a BIG word and a HARD concept for children who always want the latest of everything. Do you ever have those days when you feel like your children are constantly saying, "I want_____, I want_____, I want_____! I need_____! The complaining and whining about everything they don't have or can't have is often wearing on a mommy. It is not always easy to help them choose to see things differently—from a Biblical perspective.

Familiarize yourself with the following verses:

"I know what it is to be in need, and I know what it is to have plenty. *I have learned the secret of being content in any and every situation,* whether well fed or hungry, whether living in plenty or in want. I can do all this through him who gives me strength." Philippians 4:12-13 NIV

"I will give thanks to you, Lord, with all my heart; I will tell of all your wonderful deeds." Psalm 9:1 NIV

> *Instead of being sad or mad about what we do not have, we should thank and praise God for what He has given to us. We should be content, not wanting more!*

ACTIVITY PROPS AND SUPPLIES:

- Balloons (two balloons that are different colors)
- 8 ½ x 11 White paper
- Black marker

SCRIPT FOR MOM...

Today we are going to talk about being CONTENT with what we **have** and choosing not to focus on what we **do not have**.

In the Bible, the apostle Paul said, "I know what it is to be in need, and I know what it is to have plenty. *I have learned the secret of being content in any and every situation,* whether well fed or hungry, whether living in plenty or in want. I can do all this through him who gives me strength." Philippians 4:12-13 NIV

Explain:

- Paul had been in a lot of different circumstances.
- There were times when he was beaten, thrown in prison and had very little to eat.
- At other times, he had much or "plenty" as our verse says.
- Paul reminds us that in each of his circumstances he made a choice to be CONTENT.
- Paul made the choice to be happy with what he did and did not have, knowing God would take care of him.
- We too can choose to be happy in the situations we are in and with what we have and do not have. It is a choice!

Explain that we all make choices every day. Give them a few examples of *choices* that you make every day. Feelings can often be a *choice*. Name a few feelings children may experience: Sadness, happiness, loneliness, anger, frustration, etc. Use yourself as an example of a time today when you had to *choose* not to get "angry" or express a bad (negative) feeling. For instance: When someone pulled out in front of your car.

Explain: The Bible tells us that all of our gifts are from above. Everything we have: our home, the food we eat, the clothes we wear, and the toys we play with, etc.—all come from God. He delights in giving us gifts and wants us to *choose* to be happy with what we have. It makes Him sad when we are not grateful and CONTENT with what He has given us.

Explain: Instead of being sad or mad about what we do not have, we should thank and praise God for what He has given to us. We should be CONTENT, not wanting more!

"I will give thanks to you, Lord, with all my heart; I will tell of all your wonderful deeds." Psalm 9:1 NIV

ACTIVITY:

- Using two different colored balloons, place a few pin holes in one of the balloons without your child knowing. Allow your child to attempt to blow up the two balloons. No matter how hard he tries, he will not be able to blow up the balloon with the pin holes. However, the balloon without the holes can be blown up with little effort. Explain: Just as the balloon with the pin holes could not be blown up no matter how hard he tried, we will never be CONTENT without God's help—no matter how hard we try. The balloon without holes could be blown up with some effort on his part. Our effort combined with God's strength enables us to choose to be CONTENT.

- At the top of an 8½ x 11 white sheet of paper write: "I will give thanks to you, Lord, with all my heart." Ask your child to help you make a list of all the things God has given your family. Talk about the ways you can praise and thank Him with your whole heart for all He has given you.

- Place the list in a location in your home so you will be reminded to *choose* to be CONTENT with all God has given you.

Prayer: *Dear God, I am sorry for the times when I make You sad because I am not happy with what I have. Forgive me for thinking about the things I do not have. Please help me to be content and praise You for all You have given me. Amen!*

DAY 2

PREP FOR MOM...

Testimony on CONTENTMENT: It was Christmas time, and we were helping our boys make their wish lists. My 7-year-old, without any hesitation, asked for an iPhone. I found myself ignoring his first request to add an iPhone to his list, but then, he brought it up again. As I replied with a simple "No," he quickly responded, "But Mom, all my friends have one!" I tried to redirect him and asked him for other items for his wish list, but he was determined. You see, his friends had something he did not have. My son's heart was discontent and unhappy because he did not have what others had. He envied them for having an iPhone—he wanted what they had!

Familiarize yourself with the following verses:

"Peace of mind means a healthy body. But jealousy will rot your bones." Proverbs 14:30 ICB

> *"Peace of mind means a healthy body. But jealousy will rot your bones."*
> *Proverbs 14:30 ICB*

"Where there is *jealousy* and selfishness, there will be confusion and every kind of evil." James 3:16 ICB

"Do you know where your fights and arguments come from? They come from the selfish desires that make war inside you. You want things, but you do not have them. So you are ready to kill and are *jealous* of other people. But you still cannot get what you want. So you argue and fight. You do not get what you want because you do not ask God. Or when you ask, you do not receive because the reason you ask is wrong. You want things only so that you can use them for your own pleasures." James 4:1-3 ICB

ACTIVITY PROPS AND SUPPLIES:

- String or plastic cord for stringing beads (Craft section of store)
- Colored beads with letters
- A wide rubber band or plain wide rubber colored bracelet
- Black permanent Sharpie marker

SCRIPT FOR MOM...

Question #1: Do you remember what we talked about yesterday? We talked about how we make *choices* every day. One of the choices is *choosing* to be CONTENT or happy with what we have— thanking God because everything we have comes from Him.

Today we are going to talk about *choosing* not to focus on what others have. Sometimes we look at what our friends have, like a new toy, new bike, electronic game, etc.—and we want it.

Question #2: What is it called when we are envious or want something a friend has?

Explain: It is jealousy. Jealousy is an attitude or feeling of resentment. We resent or dislike our friend because he has something we do not have.

The Bible says, "Peace of mind means a healthy body. But jealousy will rot your bones." Proverbs 14:30 ICB

Jealousy is not a good thing, is it? Explain: When we are feeling or showing an unhappy or angry desire to have what someone else has, we are jealous of them. When we have jealousy in our hearts, the Bible tells us it rots the bones. Just like our bones in our body have to be healthy to grow, we have to be healthy so we can grow in our relationship with God. We can't grow to be who God wants us to be or have CONTENTMENT when there is jealousy in our hearts.

Question #3: Have you ever been envious or jealous of something someone else had? What was it they had that you wanted?

Question #4: Did being jealous make you feel happy or sad? Good or bad?

Question #5: Did you know that the Bible says that being jealous can cause a war inside your heart?

Read: "Do you know where your fights and arguments come from? They come from the selfish desires that make war inside you. You want things, but you do not have them. So you are ready to kill and are jealous of other people. But you still cannot get what you want. So you argue and fight. You do not get what you want because you do not ask God. Or when you ask, you do not receive because the reason you ask is wrong. You want things only so that you can use them for your own pleasures." James 4:1-3 ICB

Explain: James says that when we want things we cannot or do not have, there is a battle that goes on inside us. God wants us to be happy with what we have. But, sometimes our hearts fail to be happy—and instead are jealous. When we are struggling with jealousy and wanting what someone else has, we should ask God to help us get rid of our selfish desires (wants), and trust Him to give us what we really need. He knows what is best for us!

ACTIVITY: *Be Content Bracelet*

- Recall what it means to be CONTENT versus being envious or jealous. Ask: How does a jealous person act when he wants what others have? What is a word you would use to describe a person who is CONTENT with what God has given him? Happy, nice, joyful, etc.

- Explain to your child that today you will be making a colorful bracelet to wear—a BE CONTENT bracelet. Each day he wears it, he will be reminded to be happy with what he has and not jealous of what others have.

- When he is complaining or whining about something he does not have and showing discontentment, you will have to take his fun bracelet away for the day. The bracelet will help him remember to be CONTENT in all situations.

- Help your child construct a colorful bracelet that spells BE CONTENT with the beads. If the beads do not have letters on them, write the letters on the beads with a black Sharpie marker. Note: A wide rubber band or plain wide colored rubber bracelet can be used in place of the plastic cord and beads.

- Allow your child to wear the bracelet. If he is being discontent, take away his bracelet. Remind him about *being content* and help him to earn it back the next day.

Prayer: *Dear God, thank you for giving me all the things that I have. Please help me to not have envy or jealousy in my heart. Help me not to whine or complain, or wish I had things I do not. Help me to "be content" and use my bracelet as a reminder. Amen!*

DAY 3

PREP FOR MOM...

Testimony on CONTENTMENT: Have you ever put a toy on the floor in front of a group of two 2-year olds? They will fight, push and scream over that one toy. For most of us, it is not our natural instinct to share our things with others—our toys!

We recently sold our home, and in the process of packing, we were discussing with our children some of the things we needed to get rid of to make the move easier. For two of our children, this was exciting, and they were helpful in putting items into three large tubs marked: sell, give away or trash. But, for one of my children, this was a struggle—these were *his* things. It was hard! We had several

> *Your children will be content to the degree you are content and generous to the degree that you are generous!*

"talks" about God giving us the things we have, and how it pleases Him when we share with others who are in need. There were some tears and a sense of discontentment because I was getting rid of his things. But, in the end, he was the one who was most excited and thankful to help sell his things at our garage sale. Your children will be CONTENT to the degree you are CONTENT and generous to the degree that you are generous!

Today we are going to talk about *choosing* to be generous with what you have. Familiarize yourself with the following verses:

"Whenever you are able, do good to people who need help." Proverbs 3:27 ICB

"It is true that serving God makes a person very rich, if he is satisfied with what he has. When we came into the world, we brought nothing. And when we die, we can take nothing out. So, if we have food and clothes, we will be satisfied with that. Those who want to become rich bring temptation to themselves. They are caught in a trap. They begin to want many foolish things that will hurt them, things that ruin and destroy people. The love of money causes all kinds of evil. Some people have left the true faith because they want to get more and more money. But they have caused themselves much sorrow." 1 Timothy 6:6-7 ICB

ACTIVITY PROPS AND SUPPLIES:

- Basket or box
- Items to giveaway

SCRIPT FOR MOM...

We have talked about choosing to be CONTENT, and today we are going to talk about *choosing* to be generous with what we have. When we are generous, we are unselfish. This means we are willing to freely share what we have with others—even those things we love!

The Bible says, "Whenever you are able, do good to people who need help." Proverbs 3:27 ICB

> **Question #1:** What are some ways we can "do good" to people who need help? Discuss ways you as a family can help the needy.
>
> **Question #2:** Are there things you have that are hard for you to share with others? What are they?

Read: "There will always be poor people in the land. So I command you to give *freely* to your brothers. Give *freely* to the poor and needy in your land." Deuteronomy 15:11 ICB

> **Question #3:** Are you selfish (refuse to share) or unselfish (share freely)? When you will not share freely, you are being selfish. Who can help you have an unselfish attitude?

Explain: One of the first words that a baby learns to say is "mine"! We are born with a selfish nature. The Bible says in the verse we just read that those who give things to others are to give *freely*. That means willingly and without expecting anything in return.

Explain: God is happy when we show love through sharing *freely* what we have with those who are in need—it pleases Him. The verse I am about to read is long—so listen closely!

"It is true that serving God makes a person very rich, if he is satisfied with what he has. When we came into the world, we brought nothing. And when we die, we can take nothing out. So, if we have food and clothes, we will be satisfied with that. Those who want to become rich bring temptation to themselves. They are caught in a trap. They begin to want many foolish things that will hurt them, things that ruin and destroy people. The love of money causes all kinds of evil. Some people have left the true faith because they want to get more and more money. But they have caused themselves much sorrow." 1Timothy 6:6-7 ICB

Explain the verse above:

- Being happy with what God has given us makes us rich—not with money, but with a feeling of CONTENTMENT and satisfaction.
- We were born with nothing, and when we die and go to heaven, we will not take anything with us.
- Money will not make us happy and contented—only God can do that!
- Chasing after money and things will wear you out! But, chasing after God will make you happy and joyful!

Explain: When we are content with what we have, we are more willing to share *freely* and unselfishly what we have with people in need. This heart attitude pleases God.

Read: "Do not forget to do good to others. And share with them what you have. These are the sacrifices that please God." Hebrews 13:16 ICB

ACTIVITY: *Closet Clean-Up*

- With your child's help, go through his room, closet and toy box and take out items he does not need and place them in the box to give to someone who needs them.
- As you do, be sure to explain and reiterate the terms *selfish*, *unselfish*, *need*, *want* and *givers* versus *takers*.
- Deliver the items to a ministry for those in need: Goodwill, Salvation Army, your church, etc. You could also sell your items in a garage sale and donate the money to a charity or ministry of choice.

Prayer: *Dear God, thank You for giving me everything I need. Please help me to be content and generous with the things I have to help others who need them more. Amen!*

DAY 4

PREP FOR MOM...

We have made many choices this week related to CONTENTMENT. We have *chosen* not to focus on what we don't have, but to be grateful for what God has allowed us to have. We have made the *choice* not to focus on what others have. And, we have *chosen* to be generous with what we have.

> *Your children will be content to the degree you are content and generous to the degree that you are generous!*

Today we are going to talk with the children about *choosing* contagious CONTENTMENT. There is something about being around a person who is truly content that is contagious-it's catchy!

Familiarize yourself with the following verses:

"In the same way, you should be a light for other people. Live so that they will see the good things you do. Live so that they will praise your Father in heaven." Matthew 5:16 ICB

"Sell the things you have and give to the poor. Get for yourselves purses that don't wear out. Get the treasure in heaven that never runs out. Thieves can't steal it in heaven, and moths can't destroy it. Your heart will be where your treasure is." Luke 12:33-34 ICB

ACTIVITY PROPS AND SUPPLIES:

- Inexpensive plain colored T-shirts (Allow child to choose his color.)
- Waterproof fabric markers
- Small bottle of Germ X Hand Sanitizer
- Small bottle of glitter

SCRIPT FOR MOM...

We have made many choices this week related to CONTENTMENT, haven't we? What have we chosen to do?

- We have *chosen* not to focus on what we don't have, but to be grateful for what God has allowed us to have.

- We have made the *choice* not to focus on what others have.
- And, we have *chosen* to be generous with what we have.

Today we are going to talk about choosing contagious CONTENTMENT.

Question #1: Do you know what the word, contagious means? It means *catchy* or *infectious*. Sometimes we get sick, and what we have is contagious. That means that others can catch what we have.

Explain: So, if we are CONTENT and happy with what God has given us, our happiness and CONTENTMENT will be contagious! It will be infectious and others will catch our CONTENTMENT!

Question #2: Have you ever been around a friend who says mean and ugly things?

If mommy (and daddy) allowed you to play with them a lot, their attitude might be contagious. You would *catch* their bad attitude and begin to say mean and ugly things. Explain that our words, our actions and our attitudes should be Christ-like.

The Bible says, "In the same way, you should be a light for other people. Live so that they will see the good things you do. Live so that they will praise your Father in heaven." Matthew 5:16 ICB

Explain: This verse tells us that we are to be light, meaning we should reflect the love and peace of Christ. When we do, others will want to know why we are so happy and CONTENT. Then we can tell them about Jesus. The way we live should draw others to Jesus.

There is something about being around a person who is truly happy and content that is contagious-it's catchy!

"Sell the things you have and give to the poor. Get for yourselves purses that don't wear out. Get the treasure in heaven that never runs out. Thieves can't steal it in heaven, and moths can't destroy it. Your heart will be where your treasure is." Luke 12:33-34 ICB

God says that we are to be generous and that anything we give or share with others will always be noticed by Him. No one can steal a generous, CONTENTED heart! When we have a heart of CONTENTMENT, His heart is happy and those around us *catch* our CONTENTMENT!

ACTIVITY: *Contagious Crafts*

- **For older children:** Using a large square piece of cardboard or an ironing board, stretch the child's T-shirt until the back is flattened. Write the following words on the back: CONTAGIOUS CONTENTMENT. Allow them to choose the color of T-shirt and waterproof fabric pen. Write in small letters on the front left upper side: Philippians 4:12-13. Allow the shirt to dry before wearing it.

- **For younger children:** *Contagious Glitter Germs:* Add the small container of glitter to the hand sanitizer. Keep the bottle out of the children's sight. Gather them around to sing a song. Before singing, apply some of the glitter Germ X to your hands only. Interact with the children according to the directions while singing the song to the tune of *Goodnight Ladies:*

  Hello, Neighbor! Hello, friend. (Wave to partner)

  What do you say? (Give a high five)

  It's going to be a (Slap thighs, clap hands)

  Happy day. (Slap hands in the air with partner's hands)

  Greet your friend. (Shake hands)

  Boogie on down. (Wiggle hips)

  Give a little bump, (Bump sides)

  And turn around. (Wave hands in the air and turn around)

- When finished, look at the hands of those singing the song. Is there glitter? Yes! Compare the passing of contagious germs when we come in contact with one another to our lesson of having a contagious CONTENTMENT that is passed on to others. Close in prayer.

Prayer: *Dear God, help me to always have a contagious contentment that is catchy for those who are around me. Help me to have a generous heart willing to share all You have given me. Amen!*

DAY 5

PREP FOR MOM...

In this week's *Mommy and Me*, we have talked about CONTENTMENT. We said contentment is the state of being contented; satisfied, not desiring more than one has, and satisfied with things as they are.

In our introduction, I mentioned that, in a world where social media is constantly at the forefront, it can be difficult to remain satisfied and content.

> *As long as our expectation is from other things, nothing but disappointment awaits us."*
> *Hannah Whitall Smith*

We have a *choice* as to how we respond to the pull of the world. This is an area in our children's lives where more is caught than taught.

Not only is it a *choice* for mommy (and daddy), but we have talked with the children this week about CONTENTMENT being a *choice* for them as well. We will review their four *choices* today.

Familiarize yourself with the following verses...

"Whenever you are able, do good to people who need help." Proverbs 3:27 ICB

"Every good and perfect gift is from above, coming down from the Father of the heavenly lights, who does not change like shifting shadows." James 1:7 NIV

ACTIVITY PROPS AND SUPPLIES:

- Journal
- Pen
- Crayons, markers and stickers

SCRIPT FOR MOM...

> **Question #1:** Do you remember what we said the word CONTENTMENT means? Being satisfied with what we have, not wanting more.

When we are satisfied, we are happy with what we have—what God has given us. We talked about making *choices* and how we can *choose* to be content.

> **Question #2:** Can you tell me the 4 choices we talked about this week related to CONTENTMENT?

- We can *choose* not to focus on what we don't have, but be grateful for what God has given us.
- We can *choose* not to focus on what others have.
- We can *choose* to be generous with what we have.
- We can *choose* contagious CONTENTMENT that others around us will catch!

Explain: We had two "Do Not's" and three "Do's" this week: Do Not focus on what we do not have and Do Not focus on what others have.

> **Question #3:** Can you name the Do's? Do be grateful for what God has allowed us to have. Do be generous (give to those in need) with what we have. Do share contagious CONTENMENT.
>
> **Question #4:** What is it called when we are envious or want something a friend has? It is jealousy.
>
> **Question #5:** What is jealousy? It is an attitude or feeling of resentment. We resent or dislike our friend because he has something we do not have. Reinforcing that jealousy is not a good thing. Jealousy in our hearts will separate us from our friends and God. It makes God sad when He sees jealousy in our hearts.

The Bible says, "Whenever you are able, do good to people who need help."
Proverbs 3:27 ICB

> **Question #6:** What were some ways we talked about that we can share what we have and do good to others in need?

Do you remember mommy asking you if you were selfish (refusing to share) or unselfish (sharing freely)? When we will not share freely, we are being selfish. Who did we say can help us have an unselfish attitude? God can.

God is happy when we are not jealous of others and when we are unselfish with our things.

Question #7: Do you remember what the word contagious means? It means *catchy* or *infectious*. We said that sometimes we get sick and what we have is contagious. That means that others can catch what we have.

Explain: So, if we are CONTENT and happy with what God has given us, our happiness and CONTENTMENT will be what? CONTAGIOUS! It will be infectious and others will catch it!

Question #8: Did you have fun this week talking about CONTENTMENT? What was your favorite activity?

ACTIVITY: *Good Gifts Journal*

- Today we are going to make a family *Good Gifts* journal. God has given us so many good gifts. In James 1:7 it says, "Every good and perfect gift is from above, coming down from the Father of the heavenly lights, who does not change like shifting shadows." (NIV) We are to not only to be CONTENT with what He has given us, we are to be thankful.

- Allow the children to decorate the journal using stickers, markers or crayons.

- Each evening at dinner, ask one family member to tell of a blessing (could be any item or situation God has provided) he is thankful for and write it in your *Good Gifts* journal. You might date it as well.

Prayer: *Dear God, Thank you for teaching me about* CONTENTMENT. *I want to always make You happy by sharing what You have given me with others. I love you! Amen!*

PART TWO:

Along the Way

Along the Way

After 40 years of wandering in the wilderness, it was finally time for the Israelites to enter the Promise Land. But, before they did, God gave them commands and laws to live by. In Deuteronomy 6:1-12, God instructed His people to obey His laws. Then He instructed them to pass along these commands to their children. God didn't want the future generations to forget how He had been faithful to fulfill His promises to Abraham by leading the people out of Egypt.

Likewise, we are to pass along God's Word to our children, so that their generation and the ones after them will remember the promises of God. In Deuteronomy 6:7-9, God gave the Israelites six specific opportunities that parents have to share God's love and His Word with their children. He said, "These commandments that I give you today are to be on your hearts. **Impress** them on your children. **Talk** about them when you sit at home and when you walk along the road, when you lie down and when you get up. **Tie them** as symbols on your hands and **bind them** on your foreheads. **Write** them on the doorframes of your houses and on your gates." (NIV) We are going to break these down and give you practical ways to pass God's Word along to your children.

IMPRESS THEM ON YOUR CHILDREN...

One practical way to impress God's Word on your children is to set aside a time during the day to read God's Word as a family. This devotional book, *Mommy and Me,* is full of great devotionals that can be used by your family. If your children are younger, you can use a Children's Bible or a family devotional book.

Something that is important to remember, however, is that the only way we can pass along God's Word is if we are spending time in it ourselves. Set aside time each day to read God's Word and ask Him to speak to you through it. What God teaches you, you can then teach your children.

TALK ABOUT THEM WHEN YOU SIT AT HOME...

There are a lot of ways to incorporate God's Word into your time at home. Making these moments happen, though, requires that you have *margins* in your schedule. Just like a piece of paper has an empty *margin* around the edges, so your life needs to have room or *edges* to just be together without having multiple commitments and places to be. It is in these *margin* moments that wonderful conversations can happen and memories can be made. Here are a few suggestions on how to incorporate God and His Word into your time at home.

- **Thankfulness Journal**—We started this many years ago after I read *One Thousand Gifts* by Ann Voskamp. All day we are surrounded by ways that God blesses us: His creation, our health, kind words spoken at just the right time, our kids behaving or getting along, good friends, etc. Once you have eyes to see the things to be thankful for, it's easy to find them everywhere. Being aware of these reminds us and our children that God cares about our day-to-day activities and that He wants to bless and give good gifts to His children. It also helps combat attitudes of entitlement.

- **Highs and Lows at Dinner**—At dinnertime have each member of the family tell their high and low from the day, Mom and Dad included. Use these as times to praise God for answered prayer or unexpected surprises and also to teach how God can work in the "low times" (hard times) too.

- **Electronics**—When discussing with your children about why they can or cannot watch a certain TV show, play a video game, or use an app on the iPad, use these times of discussion as teachable moments to reinforce how everything we watch and listen to should bring God glory. Also, remind them that what goes into our minds directly affects our thoughts and actions. "Finally, brothers and sisters, whatever is true, whatever is noble, whatever is right, whatever is pure, whatever is lovely, whatever is admirable—if anything is excellent or praiseworthy—think about such things." Philippians 4:8 (NIV) Important to note: We should lead by example. If our kids see us watching an inappropriate show, then they will be confused because we are not living out what we have taught them.

- **Sibling Fights**—When a fight occurs, it is a good time to remind them that we are to be kind to one another and put others before ourselves.

- **Prayer**—Pray together for others who are sick or struggling.

- **Music**—Music can provide a fun time as a family to dance and sing. It can be a kids praise song such as Hillsong or your favorite Christian artist. Turn off the TV and play praise music while everyone reads or the children play a game. Also, you can keep Christian music playing on the radio or iPod while you cook, clean, etc. Your children will learn the songs. Often God uses songs to bring us closer to Him and to remind us of different aspects of His character.

- **Share your personal testimony**—You and your spouse can share with your kids when you accepted Christ and how God changed your life. Write down your testimony so your children will have it after you are gone.

- **Share what God is showing you in your personal quiet time** with Him each day. Include your failures and times when God has convicted you of a specific sin in your life. (Be discreet based on the age of your children.)

- **Say, "I am Sorry"**— Be willing to apologize when you have done wrong. None of us is perfect. When we ask for and receive forgiveness, it is a picture of how God forgives us when we ask. You are setting a good example for your children when you acknowledge wrongdoing and apologize.

- **A Good Name**—Spend time talking about what it means to "have a good name" and try to elevate our "name" as much as possible. Example: We do things the right way because we are Savages and Savages are honest even when it's hard, etc.

- **Word of the Day**—Our nine-year-old came up with the idea of a Word of the Day bag. She wrote words like kindness, love, courage, brave, etc., on index cards and put them in a brown lunch sack. Each day we draw one out and talk about how we can live that word out that day. Then I try to check back with them after school to see how they lived it out.

- **Value Books**—Read books as a family or listen to an Audiobook with Christian themes for discussion on practical life issues and circumstances.

- **When God Shows Up**—I have three boys and what boy does not like to pick up rocks! We will gather rocks from places we have been. In our living room, there is a large glass jar and a plate of rocks next to the jar. Anytime **God Shows Up** in our lives we write it down on a rock as a spiritual marker in our lives. A marker might be an answer to prayer or just something amazing that God has revealed to us. We want to make sure to remember these times. The rock is then placed in the jar. By writing these markers down, we not only get to see our jar fill up but it is a constant reminder to us as a family of all that God has done in our lives.

WHEN YOU WALK ALONG THE WAY...

Every day we spend time going places and these times can be used to remind our children of God's work in our daily lives. But remember, these times will not happen without purposely placing *margins* into your everyday schedule. Here are a few **"walk along the way"** ideas:

- **Hiking in the woods**—Find a park nearby or a State or National Park. Most are free and have trails that are short and great for children. Some of our greatest conversations as a family happen in the woods. I think God created us to commune with Him in a special way when we are experiencing nature. There are no distractions (phone, computer, TV, etc.). Hiking together is a great opportunity to point out God's creation and the beauty, order, and creativity of it. Psalm 19:1 "The Heavens declare the glory of God; the skies proclaim the work of His hands." NIV

- **Go for a walk in the neighborhood**—This is also a good time for talking. Our kids often share about their day or things they need to talk out on these walks. I've been doing this since they were babies. You don't have to go far or walk fast. It is a great time for sharing biblical truths and principles. My youngest calls this a *Walk and Talk*.

- **Outdoor Play**—Shoot baskets, hit the baseball, etc. Playing together is a good time to talk, laugh and have fun.

- **In the Car**—There are several things you can do in the car to remind your children of God's presence: Use the time to memorize scripture, sing praise music, and pray for the people involved when you see a fire truck or ambulance with its lights on. Morning car time is a great time to find out what your children have going on that day so you can be praying for them. Remember to ask how their day went when you pick them up. Also, it is a good time to talk about whatever is going on in their lives—but this will not happen if mom is distracted on her i-Phone!

- **Serve Together**—Examples of serving together include: Going to a local soup kitchen, helping an elderly neighbor, leaving hand written notes with candy and a big poster board sign for the trash men and postman at Christmas, letting your children help you plan and prepare a meal for someone in need, etc. I always tell our children to look for God in their day. We ask the Holy Spirit to show us where He is working and how we can help in God's plan. It is their "purpose" for each day to look for ways to share Christ by serving others.

- **Date Night**—Be deliberate in taking each child on a "date" or night out on a rotating basis. This is helpful, especially if you have multiple children, in giving them individual time away from everyone else and you will be amazed by what you find out!

- **God Sighting**—Encourage the children to find a *God Sighting* every day. A *God Sighting* is something that reminds us that God is always with us and showing Himself to us. Examples of a *God Sighting* would be a rainbow, sunbeams coming out of clouds, cows on a farm, flowers, and so on. While driving, ask them to look for a *God Sighting*. Soon they will offer up *God Sightings* without any prompting.

When you lie down...

There is something sweet about bedtime. It can be a great time for conversation about many things—including spiritual things. In an effort to postpone the inevitable, children are more apt to talk about their day, feelings, etc., at bedtime.

- **Bible Time before Bed**—When the kids were little, we would read them a Bible story at night and pray. Now we do more of a study with a theme. Some examples are: The Jesse Tree at Christmas, reading a biography of a missionary, a chronological Bible study, studying the book of Genesis through *Answers in Genesis*, etc. There are a lot of great devotionals available. We studied the Bible chronologically as a family. The kids took turns drawing what the story was for that night on a big sheet of white paper that I had divided into squares.

- **Scripture Cards**—Two of our children went through phases where they struggled with fear. My mom had the idea to buy index cards on a spiral ring. Written on each card was a scripture relating to fear. These were very comforting to my kids. They kept them by their bed and read them when they were fearful. They are older now but still use them!

- **Nighttime Reading**—Read through a book with each child individually. Take one night a week to read a chapter in a book specifically chosen for that child. Make this a time just for the two of you. Many biblical principles can be taught in these "individual" reading times.

- **4 P Bed Time**—One of my favorite things to do is putting my kids to bed. We ask if there is anything we can pray about. Once we pray with them we take about 5-10 minutes with each one to go over his day. We ask each one the 4 Ps. What was your **P**EAK of the day? What was your **P**IT of the day? What is something we could **P**RAY for today? What is something we can **P**RAISE God for today? This is when things are revealed that might not normally come out if you just ask, "How was your day?"

- **You are Awesome**—When I leave their bedrooms, I tell them, "God has made you so awesome!! He has GREAT and MIGHTY plans for you!!" I want my kids to know that as long as they are breathing God has a purpose and a plan for their lives! It is so important to constantly speak truth into their lives!

WHEN YOU GET UP...

Even though mornings can be hectic, it doesn't take but a minute to include God into the morning conversation and routine.

- **Each morning**—Ask what they have going on that day and commit to pray for them. Ask them at the end of the day about those things, reminding them of how you prayed for them and how God answered. Also, when God doesn't answer the way we want Him to, talk about how even when life doesn't go our way, God is still working and caring about us. He knows best!

- **Armor of God**—Beginning when my children were very little, we would start each day by putting on the armor of God. We would pretend to put on the helmet of salvation, then the breastplate of righteousness, and the belt of truth. Then we would lift up the shield of faith, take the sword of the spirit, and lastly pretend to put on the shoes fitted to share God's love. I would always ask them, "Why do we put on God's armor?" They would respond, "So we can be ready for our day." We still put on our armor every day on our way to school.

- **Morning Music**—Music is great for the mornings too. Calming, fun, uplifting Christian music is a great way to lift tired spirits and get everyone moving. A little dancing in the kitchen makes the day start better.

- **Breakfast Together**—When the weather is nice, my younger two girls like for us to eat breakfast together on the deck. It is amazing what spiritual conversations can occur over breakfast.

- **Notes for Lunch**—Each day I write little notes and put them in my kids' lunches. You can write them on post-it notes or just do it on the napkin. It doesn't have to be fancy. Use these notes to share scripture and to let them know you are praying for their day.

TIE THEM AS SYMBOLS ON YOUR HANDS AND BIND THEM ON YOUR FOREHEAD. WRITE THEM ON YOUR DOORFRAME AND YOUR GATES...

The Bible Hub explains the verse in Deuteronomy this way:

"God seems to have appointed, at least for the present, that some select sentences of the law that were most weighty and comprehensive, should literally be written upon their gates and walls or on slips of parchment, to be worn about their wrists, or bound upon their foreheads.

The spirit of the command, however, and the chief thing intended, undoubtedly was, that they should give all diligence and use all means to keep God's laws always in remembrance, as men frequently bind something upon their hands, or put something before their eyes, to prevent forgetfulness of a thing which they much desire to remember."

In other words, God's Word should always be in front of us guiding us and our children throughout the day. So how can we keep God's Word always before our children without writing them on their foreheads? Here are some ideas that I or my friends have used to help our families not forget God's Word.

- **Verse of the Year**—I select a verse for our kids for each school year. We spend our family Bible time that week talking about the verse and how they can apply it to the experiences they will have at school during the coming year. For instance, one year our verse was "Be strong and courageous. Do not be afraid; do not be discouraged, for the Lord your God will be with you wherever you go." Joshua 1:9 (NIV) Off and on all year we talked about how they could be courageous for God and how He would strengthen them for all they had to do. I wrote the verse on our chalkboard in the kitchen and it stayed there for the entire school year.

- **A Verse for each Child**—I also select verses that are specific to each child and pray those verses for him. I write them in my prayer journal and then share the verse with that child.

- **Bible Memorization**—Write favorite verses you are trying to memorize as a family on post-it notes and place them on your bathroom mirror or refrigerator.

- **Bring God's Word into everyday conversations** including correction and discipline. God's Word applies to all aspects of our lives. My friend, Amanda, says, "I try to use real world examples whenever possible. When friends and family members (without using their names or specifics) have something going on in their lives, I will tie scripture in that relates to the circumstances or experience."

- **Try to use God's Word** in simple daily activities and events. Example: When we plant flowers, I talk about how we have weeds in our life (sin) and how God sent His Son to take away those weeds and make us clean. Once we make God the leader of our life, we need to grow in Him. Just like a seed needs water, good soil, and sunshine to grow, we need things to grow as a Christ follower. We need His Word, prayer, and so on. Using everyday things to relate back to Christ helps the children to look at things in a different way. I try to find ways to always point them back to Christ.

- **Stones to Remember**—We collect stones when we go on vacation or to the park or hiking with friends. The children and I will write a scripture reference on one side and the names of those we were with on the other side. The stones are placed in a bowl on our kitchen table. Before dinner, we choose one and pray for the person whose name is on that stone. If we have time, we will read the scripture.

- **A Home Filled with the Word**—Collect framed scriptures pieces to place in bookcases, on walls, and in your children's rooms. Having God's Word ever before you will change the atmosphere of your home and be a witness to those who enter your house.

Bible Translations

Scripture taken from the NLT Holy Bible, *New Living Translation*, Copyright © 1996, 2004, 2015 by Tyndale House Foundation. Used by permission of Tyndale House Publishers Inc., Carol Stream, Illinois 60188. All rights reserved.

Scripture taken from The Holy Bible, *New International Version*®. Copyright © 1973, 1978, 1984, International Bible Society. Used by permission of Zondervan Bible Publishers.

Scripture taken from the Holy Bible, *New International Version* Study Bible, Copyright © 1973, 1978, 1984 by International Bible Society. Used by permission of Zondervan Bible Publishers.

Scripture taken from the Holy Bible, *New Life Version* Copyright © 1969 by Christian Literature International/ ICB The Holy Bible, International Children's Bible® Copyright © 1986, 1988, 1999, 2015 by Tommy Nelson™, a division of Thomas Nelson. Used by permission.

Scripture taken from the *New American Standard Bible*®, Copyright © 1960, 1962, 1963, 1968, 1971, 1972, 1973, 1975, 1977, 1995 by The Lockman Foundation. Used by permission.

Scripture taken from the Holy Bible, *The Living Bible* (TLB), *The Living Bible* copyright © *1971 by Tyndale House Foundation*. Used by permission of Tyndale House Publishers Inc., Carol Stream, Illinois 60188. All rights reserved.

Scripture quotations are from the ESV Bible (The Holy Bible, *English Standard Version*), copyright © 2001 by Crossway Bibles, a publishing ministry of Good News Publishers. Used by permission. All rights reserved.

Scripture taken from the Holy Bible, *International Children's Bible*® Copyright © 1986, 1988, 1999, 2015 by Tommy Nelson™, a division of Thomas Nelson. Used by permission.

Scripture taken from *The Message*. Copyright © 1993, 1994, 1995, 1996, 2000, 2001, 2002. Used by permission of NavPress Publishing Group.

About the Author

DIANNE DOUGHARTY

CHRIST-FOLLOWER—Dianne walks in sweet communion with the Lord Jesus Christ depending on Him not only for salvation but also for the empowerment for victorious Christian living.

WIFE—Dianne has been married to her high school sweetheart, Mark Dougharty, a businessman and later a minister, for forty-four years, Mark is her greatest supporter, prayer warrior, and encourager even while battling a serious illness.

MOTHER—Dianne and Mark have two daughters, Angela and Kelly.

GRANDMOTHER—Her seven delightful grandchildren call her Mimi.

DISCIPLEMAKER—For twenty years, Dianne has faithfully led Bible studies and been a speaker at women's conferences offering the truth of God's Word as the source for living the Christian life.

MENTOR—The founder of the Secrets Savored Ministry, Dianne has been a mentor for the young and the mature alike. She longs to see older women fulfill the mandate given in Titus 2:3-4 to live purposefully by making an eternal investment in the lives of young women and desires that young women become seekers of Christ, students of God's Word, and lovers of their family.

AUTHOR—Dianne is the author of the curriculum for the Secrets Savored Ministry and contributes regularly to the Missional Motherhood and My Corner Chair blogs.

secrets Savored

Secrets Savored is a mentoring ministry that is reaching this generation through practical homemaking tips and spiritual insights. Following the Titus 2 model, older women equip younger women to make their homes and families a priority. This in-depth Bible Study is also growing women into a deeper faith and building Christ-like character within them.

To order Secrets Savored books access Secrets Savored web-site at **secretssavored.org.**

·

follow us >> 🅕 📷 🐦 🅟   @secretssavored

Made in the USA
Lexington, KY
27 May 2017